FLOUR SACK SHIRTS
& HOMEMADE JAM

All the best
Enjoy the book
Ralph Hatley

FLOUR SACK SHIRTS

& HOMEMADE JAM

*Stories of a Southern
Sharecropper's Son*

Bill Holley

BUCKING CALF BOOKS

Flour Sack Shirts & Homemade Jam

© Copyright 2013 by Bill Holley

Cover photo illustrations: © Fotosearch.com/Bill Holley
© iStockphoto.com/Bill Holley

Editorial Consultants: Beverly Holley
Debbie Holley

Proofreading: Sherry Hames

Book & Cover Design: Bill Kersey

Consulting and Support: Billie Brownell
Tom Robinson

Public Relations & Marketing: Randy Guidry & Debbie Holley
Holley•Guidry PR/Mktg/Mgmt

Composed in the United States of America.

ISBN: 978-0-9895053-0-7

Paperback printed and distributed by: IngramSpark

Bucking Calf Books
P.O. Box 184
Franklin, TN 37065-2873
Phone: 239 240 6467

To my mother Naomi Ruth Crabtree Holley
The greatest gift my mother ever gave me was teaching me to read by the time I was 4.

"*It is good to love many things, for therein lies the true strength, and whosoever loves much, performs much, and can accomplish much, and what is done in love is well done.*"

Vincent van Gogh

ACKNOWLEDGEMENTS

A very special thank you to:
Beverly, Debbie, Randy, Lori and Tracy...

my beautiful and patient family.

My best girl Beverly tirelessly read story after story, critiqued, proofed and proofed again, pushed me, cheered me on, heartened me and prayed for me. After 51 years, I still see the beautiful, young, brown-eyed, brunette practicing her typewriting lessons on the big front porch of her family home in West Nashville.

To my daughter Debbie: Thank you for the countless hours spent going over each and every aspect of the stories. Without your dedication there would be no book.

To my daughter Lori: Thanks for all the prayers and the belief that I could actually write a book.

I would like to express my appreciation to the numerous people who provided support, read stories, listened to stories, offered remarks, allowed me to utilize their comments, assisted in proofreading, design, editing and generally saw me through this book.

Some of you include, by name, friend and designer Donna Richmond, friend and writer Kerry Oliver and friends and neighbors Barbara Daugherty and Bonnie Coplin. And all the kind and gentle souls who reside down Foxwood Lane. With sincere gratitude, I thank all of you.

To The Good Cup and Fido coffee shops where I found it so easy to escape life's daily chaos and write amidst the quiet storm of patrons voices. The atmosphere and the essence were inspiring.

To all those who have traveled through life with me in some shape, form or fashion and whose names I have neglected to mention, I heartily thank you.

CONTENTS

INTRODUCTION

My love for reading, my love for writing and my love for books emerged from my mother's gift of teaching me to read at a very early age. Because of that gift, I have been to places I would have otherwise never been afforded a visit. I have peeked behind the curtain; experienced other continents, countries and states; wars and love affairs; crimes and espionage; and lifestyles and cultures. I have viewed the world through the eyes of celebrities, heroes, politicians and entrepreneurs. I have been enlightened by philosophies and perspectives and opened my mind, my heart and my spirit to windows of time and the divine expectations of my Maker. It has been a gift that has continued to give year after year, and one that I treasure.

The stories just ahead are taken from my life as a sharecropper's son from age four to fourteen. Putting them on paper came from my desire to leave a written history of my rural youth for my two city-raised daughters, "Boo" (Debbie) and "Pokey" (Lori), or "Shortie" and "Peanut," respectively, as my father affectionately referred to them. I simply wanted to document for them my early years on the farm and a way of life that is rapidly starting to fade.

Sharecropping was a hard life that made for rough, work-worn hands and sore bent backs but it also built a work ethic of honesty, and a belief in fair dealing. It was a family affair everyone had to pull his or her weight and contribute. *An honest day's work for an honest day's pay.* A cliché, true, but it was the reputation that my dad had with all those who knew him.

Clyde and Naomi Crabtree Holley were my parents. My dad was industrious, inventive and virtually indefatigable. He was practical, straightforward, tough-minded and plainspoken, and, from my standpoint, a strict and harsh disciplinarian with a handy razor strap.

My mother was grit and grace with a heartbeat. She worked as hard as any man, then turned around and loved everyone around her selflessly. From the flour sack shirts and dresses she sewed to the homemade jam she made from growing, picking, canning and storing fruits; her resourcefulness, initiative and originality seemed endless. Her culinary creations were a special treat to the entire community, and her patterns, handiwork and crafts as skilled and creative as anything I've encountered since. Where dad was tough and unbending, my mother was gentle, kind and compassionate, although she did keep a peach-tree switch nearby, and knew how to use it.

What I had was hard-working parents with calloused and blistered hands who provided me with everything that I really needed. Once in a while, play and fun replaced work. Rainy days, Saturday afternoons and Sundays after church were times set aside to relax and re-wind, visit neighbors and friends with my parents or walk the hills and valleys. A complementary, yet conspicuously opposite pair they were, but together they created a sense of balance in my life.

To my young mind, being *sharecroppers* meant that we were *poor folks*. There were times when I was ashamed that I didn't have the clothes, toys or spending money that some of the kids of our more affluent farm neighbors had. And naturally, there were always a few in every community who looked down their nose at us, holding us accountable for the life we were born into. While that same few might have been dismayed by our lack of wealth, even they couldn't find fault with hard work and a harvest reaped. My parents were quick to dismiss their haughtiness as ignorance.

We moved many times, and with each move we made new friends, but remained connected to our former neighbors. For me, each new community provided new faces, new experiences and new adventures. There always seemed to be someone in the community who became a mentor to me, a special person who challenged and pushed me to be and do more with my life than I thought I ever could. To those wonderful people I say a heartfelt thank you!

Over time, and at the expense of the years ticking away with real-time experiences, our definitions of certain things change, and certainly our perspectives transform and adjust. Now when I look back, it's like looking through a giant kaleidoscope filled with engaging people, places and establishments in colors that are bigger, brighter and bolder.

I'm proud and I smile, AND I see only a very charmed life.

FLOUR SACK
SHIRTS
& HOMEMADE JAM

HEAVENLY DOLLOPS:
JAMS, JELLIES & PRESERVES

"Mother's love is peace. It need not be acquired, it need not be deserved."
— *(Author Unknown)*

It MAY be as simple as a biscuit and a dollop of blackberry jam.
—*(Bill Holley)*

I was born and raised out in the country, the rural South, God's country, in my estimation. My parents were sharecroppers. It was a time long past when the air was still fresh, and in the summertime, the rolling hills and valleys were green and lush, the farms well-tended. It was back when you could still safely drink from a spring branch and man's relationship with nature was understood and not a political agenda.

Food was fuel for the hard farm work, but no less tasty for it, and a good hearty breakfast was a necessary start for each day. Time spent around the breakfast table figures prominently in my memories and the romantic recall of my youth.

No farm breakfast would ever have been complete without piping hot, made-from-scratch buttermilk biscuits slathered with freshly churned sweet cream butter and smeared with a big dollop of Mother's, or my grandmother Ma's, homemade jams, jellies or preserves.

Those delicious home-produced sweets came at a price: hot summer days in the wild blackberry patch fighting briars, chiggers, wasps, sunburn and the occasional snake, and sometimes, when picking in a neighbor's pasture, dodging their Jersey bull and his naturally nasty disposition. Peaches came with their own set of challenges when earmarked for the cut-glass preserve stand or the pint glass Mason jars. With peaches you found yourself dodging the bullet stings of the honeybees swarming around the overripe and rotting peaches below the trees. Harvesting pears usually called for tree-climbing skills and tight-wire balance as you shook the limbs from high above the ground.

BLACKBERRY PICKING

Nearly every farm's cow pasture had at least one wild blackberry patch. Those juicy blackberries, full of seeds, would ripen during the hottest time of the year when the chiggers were the most abundant and their hungriest. On berry-picking day, as soon as the daily chores at the barn and house were complete, Mother would put on a pair of Dad's old overalls, a long sleeved shirt and her big floppy straw hat, the one with the faded flowers painted on the hatband. Her outfit served to protect her from scratches, but mostly it was to keep her from getting a suntan. Suntans were not really popular back then, especially with farm wives who didn't want to be considered "redneck." Women were supposed to be fair of skin, but no farmer's wife ever saw the luxury of sitting in the shade all day fanning every breath and sipping on lemonade.

I dressed in my usual: faded overalls, a homemade cotton flour-sack shirt and work shoes. I grabbed my own stained and tattered straw hat, positioned it firmly on my head, and readied myself for some serious berry pickin.' Our berry pickin' outfits complete, Mother commenced to swabbing our wrists and ankles with coal oil-soaked rags, and then she tied them around our wrists and ankles. This was supposed to ward off the imminent chigger attack, or at least limit the assault. If the assaults I was the victim of were limited, I'd hate to see the damage the entire army of chiggers could do. Gangs of those darn critters always managed to high-jump the coal oil barriers, and when I returned home, I was itching from head to toe and covered in the tiny despicable red creatures.

Finally we were off, down the cow path and across the pasture to the big blackberry patch, Mother toting a big milk bucket for collecting berries, and me armed with a gallon molasses bucket for gathering. As soon as we reached the patch, I promptly started picking berries. My mouth watered more with every one that I selected, and soon I was unable to resist temptation. I ate about one of every three that I picked. "Billy, if you keep eating the berries, you won't ever get your bucket filled, son," Mother scolded. "Besides they need to be washed before you eat any. They might have tiny bugs or spiders on them that won't come off by you just blowing on them." This was just another day of hard work for Mother, but at my young age it was quite an adventure. I always looked forward to picking berries with my mother. It was a time when she shared stories of her early life with me, like how she helped her dad with the family farm.

She told stories about her older sister Louise; how she and Louise walked 2 miles each way to attend the one-room Albright School. Stories about when she worked at her Uncle Clabe Crabtree's grocery store testing eggs for fertility, using a procedure called candling, and spinning cream from milk using a cream separator. She talked about her boyfriends. She told stories about her extended family; her mother had 11 brothers and sisters, so there was plenty to talk about. She told me how she met Dad at an Albright School box supper. He bid on and bought her box of fried chicken, country ham, homemade biscuits and apple pie. Dad was working as a farmhand on a Tennessee general farm that joined the Crabtree family property. He had just returned from Bono, Arkansas, where he had lived and worked on a cotton farm.

She stepped back for a moment and told me how she and Dad married, reciting their wedding vows while sitting in a one-horse buggy, and how they survived the Great Depression, living mostly on poke salad, hog meat, eggs, white beans and Irish potatoes.

Occasionally Dad would join us in the berry patch, but he really had neither time, nor the patience, for blackberry picking. The bucket didn't fill quickly enough for him, and if he couldn't see progress in rapid motion, he had no use for whatever the task might be.

The biggest, plumpest berries were always in the middle of or the backside of the patch, and we had to trample the vines to get to the prize berries. The thorns tore at our clothes and scratched our faces, arms and legs. Oh, but it was worth every battle scar. Then, the black racer and green snakes always seemed to be where you least expected them, usually where you were just about to step, or right where you were about to reach for an especially big berry. Even with the best berries and in a good year, it seemed to take forever to fill our pails, but eventually time clicked away, and our buckets were overflowing with ripe, juicy blackberries. Simply nothing is quite as sweet and succulent as a freshly picked black-berry right out of the pail, and even after Mother's warning about bugs, I still sneaked a few.

Scratched and bleeding, clothes torn, itching from gazillions of chigger bites, and soaked with sweat, there we were, proudly parading with pails full of blackberries and smiles on our faces, walking down the cow path back to the house. A cow path always seemed to be close to every blackberry patch.

We untied the rags from around our ankles and wrists and removed some of our dirty berry-picking garb, which was covered in cockleburs and stick-tights, leaving the rags in a separate pile from the clothes just outside the back door. Back in the kitchen, my first order of business was to wash a cup of berries, sprinkle them with sugar, add a little milk cool from the spring, and proceed to eat my fill of those delicious, dark, juicy fruits of our morning trip to the berry patch.

AND SO THE PROCESS BEGAN...

Canning Blackberries for Cobbler...
and Making Blackberry Jam and Jelly

The day before our berry pickin' adventure, Mother had retrieved a number of glass, pint and quart Mason jars and lids from our root cellar out back of the house where she had stored them. She would use the quart jars for berries cooked for cobblers and the pint jars for preserves, jam and jelly. She carefully washed the dust and spider webs from the jars, and placed new rubber seals for the lids nearby. Mother organized and set up her work-station on the kitchen table.

While I ate berries until my lips, my tongue and my shirt were stained purple, Mother put a dishpan of water on the stove to heat, and placed the jars in the water long enough to warm, then removed them. She heated the jars to keep them from cracking when she poured in the molten fruit mixture.

Mother dumped the berries into her large, white enamel dishpan and covered them in cold water. She washed the fruit clean of bugs, sticks, leaves and any other foreign matter. After washing and draining the berries, Mother carefully poured them into cooking pots, adding "just the right amount" of water and sugar, after which she placed the pots on the hot stovetop.

The heat in the kitchen could reach sweltering levels when these sweet concoctions were being prepared, and canning was taking place. Our house had a wood-burning cook stove, and no air conditioning. We didn't have electricity until I was 7 or 8 years old. An open window and a prayer for a cool breeze were all we could hope for.

When the fruit boiled down to "just the right consistency" for cobbler, Mother filled the quart jars. The other pots, still on the stove, continued to cook, and when the berries were "cooked down just right" for jam or jelly, she carefully poured the molten mixture into the pint jars. "Just right" was a judgment call. There was no timer or temperature gauge on the wood-burning cook stove and no thermometer to measure the heat of the boiling berry mixture, just hard-earned judgment and experience passed down from generation to generation or friend to friend.

Peach Preserves from the Peaches In Pa's Orchard

Peach preserves were made much the same way as blackberry jam and other fruit preserves, with hard work, sweat and a bit of Mother's and Ma's cooking magic.

Each summer of my childhood, I stayed a week with my grandparents. Early some mornings, I would tag along barefoot with my granddad to the orchard that covered almost 5 acres behind his big stock barn. Picking fruit was a morning chore. Plenty of obstacles and obstructions were on the way to the peach orchard; most of the time you had to walk across grass lots and pastures filled with nettles, briars and locoweed. A barefoot boy had to dance a careful jig to avoid going on with his feet full of stickers.

Ripening season for peaches was the hot summertime, and the ground underneath the trees was always carpeted with ripe and rotting peaches. The orchard was fragrant, smelling sweet and tangy as nature took its course and the peaches fermented in the heat of the summer sun. The ground was covered with honeybees buzzing about, each with a spiteful disposition. I always ran barefooted during the summer, and it resulted in more than my share of bee stings.

My granddad Pa reigned king over his orchard, and most every year the limbs of his fruit trees were loaded down almost to the breaking point. From a distance, it looked as though they were stretching their branches and reaching for the ground, perhaps weary from the weight of their load.

We picked the peaches off the trees and gingerly placed them in the small, split-oak fruit baskets, careful not to bruise them. There were the big peaches that were great for eating, but not so good for making peach preserves. And then, Pa's orchard had several trees that produced a smaller, more firm, almost hard peach with a lot of acid. Those were the peaches that made magnificent peach preserves.

We worked to fill our baskets, always taking at least one basketful of the big juicy freestone peaches to set out on Ma's kitchen counter to grab and eat when the notion struck us. Those big, juicy, freestone Elberta "eating peaches" were fleshy, deep yellow and rich with fragrance and flavor. Fuzzy on the outside, the fruit was sweet on the tongue with a light burst of acid, and they grew the size of softballs. A juicy tree-ripened peach will delight the senses like no other fruit in nature's collection. They're best right off the tree and slightly warm from the sun or right out of the basket in Ma's kitchen at room temperature.

Some of my fondest memories are those made going with Pa to the orchard. "Billy, Ma's gonna be looking for us directly with these peaches in tow," Pa would say. "She'll skin our hides if we don't get back pretty soon, but I think we'd be missin' out a right smart if we don't sit down and eat us one of these big ones right now, don't you?" "I sure do, Pa," I'd answer him. "Pick you one out, son," he'd add.

I'd pick a big ripe peach off the tree and hand it to Pa. We'd sit down under the tree, lean back against the knotty trunk, and he'd peel it with his old, worn Case pocketknife. We'd share slices of that wonderful fruit, one for you, one for me, sweet and sticky peach juice dripping from our fingers. We caught the juice with a swipe of the backs of our hands across our chins as it trickled down. God sure knew what he was doing when he made *some* fruit for making jam, jelly and preserves and *some* fruit for eating.

My granddad Pa was also a master beekeeper. His exceptional ability with honeybees seemed to be innate, a "bee whisperer" of sorts. The honeybees lived in my granddad's beehives at the edge of the orchard, and the orchard was a favorite spot for them to hang out.

Pa's bees went to work early in the spring, and he harvested at least two lard stands full of the liquid gold. Deep and rich in color, the honey and its accompanying waxy honeycomb was the architectural handiwork of the honeybees each season.

Left to their own, honeybees coexist with their surroundings, including man, quite easily, but several times each summer, those fuzzy, little black-and-yellow bees morphed into winged aggressors when I invaded their territory and distracted them from their work. The bees could be quite liberal with their stings, but it was only when I disturbed them that they popped me with a fury and without prejudice.

They were never discriminating about the location of the stings, nor were they conservative in the number of times they stung, often catching me on my bare feet, arms, hands or my head. For most country folks, applications of moist baking soda or a bit of moist chewing tobacco were the best remedies for bee stings, although most kids cringed at having a piece of wet tobacco placed on their arm or leg and even more so if it was taken right out of the mouth of the chewer and pulled directly from his or her chaw-in-progress. When Pa finished "robbing" the hives, he sometimes encouraged the bees to sting his knuckles. He claimed that the stings helped his rheumatism.

Pear Preserves and the Art of "Chewy"

Pear preserves. Sweet and chewy, with a texture like no other and a wonderful consistency. They were quite possibly my favorite, if my arm was twisted to name one, at the breakfast table.

At times during the summer we would go for a Sunday drive, usually to look for hay to buy. Sometimes we took a ride to look at the scenery or just get out of the house awhile. While riding through the countryside, we would occasionally spot an old pear tree or two out in a cow pasture or along the edge of a neighbor's garden, sometimes along the side of the road, and every so often in an orchard, their limbs bending with fruit. Mother and

Dad would always make a note of the location. They weren't shy about driving right up to the property owner's house and asking if they would sell some of the pears. Some refused, but an amazing number agreed; money was hard to come by back then, and every little bit helped.

Pears were always a bit easier to gather than blackberries. At least they were ready for picking later in the year, around the time of the first frost of autumn when the weather was certainly a little cooler. We usually ended up picking three or four burlap feed bags full when the pears were ready.

Country folks just called them old-fashioned cooking pears. They were hard, with a good amount of acid, and they were also sweet and tasty and had a sort of crispy crunch if you bit into one. I was continually cautioned by all of the grown-ups that over-eating the hard fruit would give me a painful stomachache, and it usually did. But the stomachache was worth the experience of that delectable fruit. The fancy, hybrid "eating pears" found at the grocery were just no good for making pear preserves. They were too soft and quickly turned to mush when cooked down. The candied goodness of pear preserves called for the tougher, more textured pear.

Dad and I usually did all of the pear picking as it meant climbing the trees and shaking the limbs vigorously until the pears fell to the ground. We did our pear picking on the weekends, most often on Sunday mornings, just about Dad's only leisure time.

Back home with our load of bulging burlap bags, we emptied some of the pears into Mothers' big galvanized washtub filled with clean, fresh water from the well or the spring. The pears were washed thoroughly, then peeled and sliced into silver dollar-sized pieces. Cores and peelings were put into a feed bucket for our pigs; those critters loved pear cores and peelings. We tossed sliced pear pieces into pots with water and sugar. A few of the pears were set aside for Mother's special family recipe for pear honey, always made in small quantities, a sort of seasonal limited-edition concoction at our house.

As with the berries, Mother knew from experience just how much sugar to sprinkle and water to add, and how long to keep the concoction boiling on the stove, so that the preserves were cooked to "just the right" chewy, gooey, candied preserve consistency. Cooked too long, they could pull out your teeth. Cooked too little, sticky pear juice would escape your biscuit and dribble down your chin to your shirtfront. When the cooking hit its peak, the pots were quickly removed from the stove, and the bubbling, scalding hot preserves were poured into pint glass jars, sealed and turned upside-down. Mmmmm, I can almost taste those chewy sweet pear preserves right now.

For jelly, the cooked fruit and juice was strained through cheesecloth and the seed pulp was thrown away. The jam was poured directly into the jars, seeds and all. Lids on all the jars were carefully screwed down tightly after placing a rubber seal ring on the lip of the jar. Then, all the jars were turned upside-down on the table to cool, a step taken to aid in the vacuum sealing of the jar. Some country cooks and skilled homemakers further ensured a tight seal by pouring melted paraffin right on top of the jam, jelly or preserves in the jar to seal it from the air before adding the rubber ring and the lid, but Mother never did. The entire process of canning berries and making jams, jellies and preserves moved with conscious rhythm like a well-choreographed production. Such kitchen precision took years of practice and fine-tuning.

The jars of jams, jellies, preserves, and pie and cobbler berries were added to row upon row of glass jars containing colorful canned fruits and vegetables. The jars filled the rough-sawed shelves that lined two walls in our root cellar. Mother and Ma canned quite a lot of food and the glowing pride of accomplishment always showed on their faces when they showed visitors the "fruits" of their summer labor. Lined up on the shelves, you could see the bright red of canned tomatoes; the deep purple-red of blackberry jam and jelly; the various shades of green string beans, lima beans, peas and turnip greens; the bright colorful mixtures of corn, tomato and green pepper relishes; the bright yellow of canned peaches; and the reddish-gold brown of the semi-transparent peach and pear preserves. I remember one particularly bountiful summer; Mother "put up" more than 300 jars of fruits and vegetables.

Ma's Cut-Glass Preserve Stand and Honey Stand

My grandmother Ma had a beautiful, square, cut-glass pedestal preserve stand that sat on the lace tablecloth in the middle of the dining room table where all of her meals were served. It was always filled with one of her homemade jams, jellies or preserves. Ma also kept a smaller honey stand filled with golden honey and honeycomb harvested from Pa's beehives.

Although they weren't a matching pair, both of Ma's pedestal stands were beautifully cut and shaped, and each was complete with its own matching top. The cut-glass facets would sparkle like jewels in the flickering light of the coal oil lamp that graced her dining table. Both had been handed down from generation to generation. Ma guessed from as far back as the 1800s but she didn't really know for sure. One thing was certain: You could always count on one of Ma's stands being filled with honey, preserves or jam.

I don't remember having a single breakfast meal at Ma and Pa's house without honey and one of those wonderfully delectable, fruity delights gracing her table. We weren't quite as fancy as Ma at our house. Mother served our home-produced breakfast sweets right out of the jars she worked so hard to fill, the fruit of her labor I suppose. Those colorful jams, jellies and preserves tasted just as good dipped straight from a canning jar as they did at Ma's, gently spooned with a silver serving spoon, from her handsome cut-glass preserve stand. At our table, Mother's spirit and smile were in every scrumptious tablespoon that I devoured; every dollop that

I swirled with precision on my hot buttery biscuit. She sealed the twinkle in her eyes and happiness in her heart in every single jar.

Mother's tender affection was neither acquired, nor conditional in form or distribution. Sometimes tangible, sometimes not. Its effects were far-reaching, and sometimes as simple as a biscuit and a dollop of blackberry jam.

— (Bill Holley)

MOTHER'S PEAR HONEY RECIPE

Yield: Makes 6 to 8 pint jars or 12 to 16 ½ pint jars

Ingredients:
   Measurements are approximate. My mother, Naomi Ruth Crabtree, rarely, if ever, measured anything.
   6 lbs. (approx. 16 cups) peeled, cored and chopped pears
   1 (20-ounce) can crushed pineapple with syrup
   10 cups of sugar (approx.)
   Juice of ½ lemon (approx. 1 tablespoon lemon juice)
   12 to 16 (½-pint) canning jars and lids or 6 to 8 (pint) canning jars with lids

Directions:

Combine all ingredients in a large saucepan. Bring ingredients to a gentle rolling boil. Cook until pears are tender and mixture thickens, approximately 30 minutes. Note: Keep in mind; the pear honey will set up, or thicken, a little upon cooling. Its consistency is spreadable in the same fashion as marmalade. Transfer to warm sterilized glass jars and seal while they're still hot. Follow instructions for sterilization, canning and processing that come with the jars or seek USDA guidelines for canning.

Candling Eggs:

Egg candling is a procedure for testing eggs for fertility. First, the room in which this work is done must be dark. You must employ an empty cardboard or wooden box with a round hole, very slightly smaller than an average hen egg, in one side of the box. There is a bright light bulb inside the box on the opposite side of the hole. When an egg is placed up to the hole on the outside of the box, the bulb backlights the egg. To the naked eye, this reveals shapes inside the egg. This allows the person doing the candling to determine if any fertilized spots or un-hatched chicks are present. Most folks have a particular aversion to eggs with a red spot on the yolk or a baby chick in the yellow.

Separating Cream From Milk:

Whole milk was placed in a "cream separator," a hand-cranked centrifuge. The whirling action actually separated the milk from the cream. The milk was drained off, and the cream was poured into small stainless steel "cream cans." The milk separated from cream, which was called "blue John" and had little or no nutritional value, was thrown away or fed to the hogs. In the days when Mother was a teenager, farmers could sell cream but not whole milk. They would bring their milk to the grocery; the store provided the separator and bought the cream for resale to cheese plants and to commercial creameries for making butter and other products.

The price of the cream was based on the butterfat content. The butterfat content was determined by a series of chemical "test tube" samples and testing procedures.

END

MISS ELLA'S HOLLYHOCKS

There were 10 wooden steps leading to the front porch of our little house on the hillside that rose from the valley. From my perch on the top step, I had an eagle's-eye view of the entire valley that spread out a half-mile in all directions, with its checkered patchwork quilt of greens, browns and golds that were the fields. Here and there were small color bursts and splashes of white, red, burgundy and the various shades of pink and purple that were the carefully tended flowers and gardens of the farm wives. These were the fields, pastures and gardens that made up the small farms of our community called Catalpa.

In my view to the left was the Catalpa Store, also known as Wade Daniel's Store, the anchor to this farming community. Wade opened the doors at 6:30 a.m. every morning and closed at 7:00 p.m. every day except Sunday. Even then, he opened at the same time but closed in time for he and his wife Edith to attend the 10:00 a.m. worship at the little white Catalpa Church of Christ. On Saturday afternoons, neighbors gathered to buy groceries, and the women-folk caught up on the latest neighborhood gossip. Farmers congregated at the store on Sunday mornings to purchase the Sunday paper, drink "Co-Colas," talk politics, farming and hunting, and (although they'd never admit to it) also to catch up on all the latest gossip.

A few yards east of the store was where our rutted and washed-out gravel road, hardly more than a wagon path, began. It wound its way south, bordered on the left side by the electric fence that ran the perimeter of Bob Murdock's crimson clover field. The road continued across the rickety old wooden bridge, over two cattle guards, past Freeman Wakefield's house and barn, through two gates and up the rutted dirt road that climbed the steep hill to our house.

If I looked to the far right through the trees that surrounded our house, I could see Mr. John and Miss Ella Watson's little white house with its rusting tin roof and their old dilapidated barn. Their little farm was nestled right near where the valley stopped and the hills began—the southeastern perimeter of the valley. All around, there were bright patches of color: hollyhocks in burgundy, pink, and red contrasting against the greens of the trees and grass and the white of the little house. Vivid colors that were a beautiful complement against the weathered, gray boards of the old barn. Miss Ella and Mr. John had lived in this house on this small farm ever since their wedding day more than 50 years before. Everyone knew her as "Miss Ella" even though she had been married to Mr. John for all those years.

My parents and I lived in a small, white two-story farmhouse that rested on the brow of the hill. In the summer that was my 6th year I would beg my mother several times a week to allow me to visit Miss Ella and Mr. John. They were a warm and welcoming old couple, and they came to dote on my visits. I walked down the hill the half-mile or so to their house, my tanned and dirty bare feet crunching the parched, brown summer grass of our cow pasture, before crossing the fields of golden stubble that had been oats, recently cut for winter hay. Before I reached my destination, I skipped and splashed my way to the other side of the narrow, winding little stream that was overhung with willows casting their cool green reflections in the deep clear pools. Large schools of silverside minnows in the shallow areas were waiting for me to play "catch me if you can." I seldom ever caught one, and if I did, it wiggled quickly from my grasp and back into the stream to rejoin its "schoolmates," and I resumed my journey.

Then, it was on through the paw-paw thicket, where I stopped long enough to test the ripeness of the bright green fruit. When ripe, you could peel back the skin of the banana-like fruit to reveal the vanilla pudding texture and color inside. The fruit had a slightly sweet, sort of pungent flavor that was uniquely its own, somewhat similar to sassafras tea, and although I wasn't overly fond of this wild Southern fruit, I would occasionally stop long enough to peel and eat one anyway.

My path continued on past the Watsons' old barn, a structure desperately fighting for its life in the never-ending battle against time and decay, and losing more battles than it won. Pieces of the tin roof were blown back by some long ago windstorm, exposing the naked ribs of wooden lathe and underneath those, the rafters. The gray boards of the barn's sides were rotting and a great many were missing, exposing the barn's interior of failing and decaying timber, rotting hay and straw. In the corner of a stable were unidentifiable, rusty pieces of machinery long since unused and forgotten. But, the barn had a certain beauty and appeal as Miss Ella's hollyhocks growing along its walls, preening in the wind, greeted me with a wave and a nod as I walked past them on my way to see Miss Ella and Mr. John. Their cheeriness was infectious, and I couldn't help but smile at them without really knowing or understanding why.

My bare feet slapped a rhythm on the final section of the packed clay path that ran from the barn to the house. I passed the little spring that bubbled enthusiastically out of the ground, the old couple's only source of drinking water. A half-gallon glass jug that once held Karo syrup that was now filled with milk sat up to its lid in the crystal spring water, keeping cool and fresh for their supper table.

I continued on around the side of the house, past Miss Ella's carefully tended flowerbeds of marigolds, zinnias, hydrangeas and tiger lilies. The path led me to the front porch, where I could usually find the old couple: Miss Ella in her rocking chair, crocheting and

Mr. John in the porch swing, musing about life in general and relating stories of his youth. Occasionally, he would ask Miss Ella to retrieve an apple and a knife from the kitchen, whereupon he would peel the apple and cut it in small sections to share with Miss Ella and me. This seemingly trivial act was an extraordinary feat for one such as Mr. John.

Mr. John was in his 80s—tall, slightly stooped and gaunt, with thinning gray hair and a drooping, slightly tobacco-stained, walrus mustache that matched the color of his hair, but for the stains. His hickory walking cane was always within his easy reach, just in case he decided to leave the swing to stretch his legs. He needed that cane to search out any obstacles that might be in his path, as Mr. John was stone blind and had been from the time he was in his 11th year. He was a victim of some unnamed childhood ailment that left him forever sightless, but the old man could "see" more with his ears, touch, smell, taste, memories and imagination than many of us will ever "see" with perfect vision and all of our senses.

Mr. John had a million stories to tell, and I would sit on the stone steps to their porch and listen for hours in rapt, wide-eyed attention, transported back to another time by his colorful yarns of ghosts and other tall tales from his youth, some true and some not. Shaking her head, Miss Ella would say, "Now, John, don't fill this child's head with more of your nonsense," and Mr. John would laugh.

Miss Ella was a mite of a woman, barely 5 feet tall, with stooped, rounded shoulders, her back bent from a lifetime of hard work, doing the best she could to scratch out a meager living for her and Mr. John. In the summer growing season, she spent long hot days, hoe in hand, chopping weeds out of her vegetable garden. Air conditioning in the Watson house was non-existent, so there was little cooling comfort after a day's gardening. My dad, a couple of other close neighbors and Wade Daniels, the amiable storekeeper, saw to it that Mr. John and Miss Ella were supplied with ice, usually a 50-pound block every few days during July and August, and the well-loved couple was never charged a penny.

She had twinkling blue eyes and white hair pulled back in a bun that she held in place with a pair of tortoiseshell combs, and she was forever tucking the ever-present loose wisps of hair behind her ears as she concentrated on the work at hand. Miss Ella's pride and joy was her big, old, church pump organ that almost filled the keeping room of their tiny house. In the quiet of summer's late evening twilight, when the breeze was just right, my mother, my dad and I would sit on our front porch and quietly listen until bedtime as Miss Ella played old cowboy songs and church hymns on that big 'ole organ, the gathering darkness punctuated by the blinking taillights of a hundred lightning bugs.

Whenever I came to visit, there always seemed to be a batch of sugar cookies (she called them "teacakes"), still warm from the oven, on Miss Ella's kitchen table along with a pitcher of fresh, cold milk or some freshly squeezed lemonade from their old wooden icebox. So as not to hurt Miss Ella's feelings, I felt that it was my bounden duty to eat my fill of those cookies and wash them down with a glass of cold milk while I listened to Mr. John weave the magic of his yarns into a colorful tapestry. I would listen and munch, Miss Ella would rock and crochet, and Mr. John would swing and talk. "Snowball," their little white ball-of-fur dog was always nearby, standing ready to mooch a cookie, and successful at doing so most of the time. Miss Ella would gently chide, "Honey, don't give him all your teacake. He's a spoiled little butterball already."

Miss Ella loved flowers of all kinds, but most of all she loved hollyhocks, those tall, bright pink, burgundy, red or white flowers with large green leaves that grew around chimney corners, along yard fences and next to the yard gates of even the poorest hard-scrabble farm. Miss Ella's hollyhocks blossomed in bright profusion along the sides of their porch, near the front and back gates, against the outside walls of their old barn, and even along the big creek that ran a few hundred feet from the front of their house. The bright colors of hollyhocks could brighten even the dullest and most dilapidated of structures, though Miss Ella's house was never dilapidated, but rather well-kept considering she had to do most of the upkeep herself. Somehow Miss Ella's hollyhocks seemed bigger, brighter and more full of life than all the others in Catalpa. They were almost animated; in fact, they nearly appeared in "Technicolor."

During one of my frequent visits, Miss Ella had her usual plate of just-baked sugar cookies waiting for me, but this time she had an additional treat in store. She left the porch for the living room, returning momentarily with an ancient tattered storybook, its cloth cover frayed and the spine pulled apart. "Billy, I found this old book yesterday while I was in the attic looking for some sheet music for the organ. My mother read this book to me when I was a little girl, and I thought you might like to hear the story of Jack and the Beanstalk if you haven't heard it before." My grandmother had read me the story more than once, but I kept that bit of information to myself, as I wanted to hear Miss Ella's version. I lay back on the porch and got comfortable, and she began, "Once upon a time..." I listened, and daydreamed, as I stared at Miss Ella's hollyhocks, pretending that they were produced from Jack's Magic Beans and that they would grow up to the sky.

Bumblebees love hollyhocks, and most 6-year-old country boys have a fascination for bumblebees; at least they did in the 1940s. I was no exception, and I watched keenly as the flying, fat critters would enter the large hollyhock flowers for the pollen— then, I would pinch the petals of the big flower together, trapping the bee inside. I would put my ear close and listen to the frantic buzzing. After a few moments, I would release my hold on the flower with the angry bee inside, then run like the devil himself was after me so I wouldn't get stung. It was instant entertainment for a 6-year-old with few friends close by to play with and driven by simple childhood curiosity. No harm done to the bee or the flower, although it was likely a bit less amusing for each of them.

On one such occasion I was running around Miss Ella's house, lickety-split, with a real or imaginary bumblebee in hot, angry pursuit. Looking back at the wrong instant as I rounded the corner of the house, I slammed full-force into one of their ancient maple shade trees. It knocked me out cold. I have no idea how long I was out, probably no more than a few seconds, but I awoke with a terrific headache, a large, purple "goose egg" on the side of my head and a tree-bark imprint on the side of my face. Trying to hold back the tears, I slowly limped the rest of the way around the house to the front porch where I shared my painful misfortune with Miss Ella and Mr. John.

Miss Ella sympathetically helped ease my pain, suffering and busted pride with a cold washcloth for my head, kind and comforting words of compassion and two fresh sugar cookies with a glass of ice-cold, homemade lemonade. Mr. John showed almost no sympathy at all and actually laughed as he contemplated my recent terrible misfortune. "That tree jump right out in front of you, did it, Billy?" asked Mr. John, as he started to spin a yarn about how once when he was a small boy not much older than me, a tree had literally jumped out in front of him. "Now John, you know that story ain't so," Miss Ella scolded, "stop filling this child's head with your nonsense."

After a while, the pain of my accident had somewhat subsided, and although the "goose egg" remained, I helped Miss Ella clean out her goldfish bowl with its bright-colored marbles and two goldfish. She let me dip the goldfish out of the bowl using a small net with a long wire handle. "Now be really careful and don't drop the little fellers," she said as I carefully placed them in a quart glass jar filled with fresh clean water. She emptied the old water from the fishbowl, removed the marbles and washed them and the inside of the bowl thoroughly; then she filled the clean bowl with fresh water before returning the little, bright-colored fish to their home. "Oh, look how happy they are in their fresh clean home; you can almost see them smiling," she said. I looked really hard, but I just couldn't see any smiles on the faces of those goldfish. The afternoon wore on, and soon it was time for me to retrace my steps along the path and head up the hill toward home.

Just like always, before I left their house, Miss Ella gave me a small brown paper sack filled with what was left of the sugar cookies. This particular time, however, she placed another smaller paper bag in my hand. It was a bag of "magic seeds" that came along with her careful verbal instructions on when and how to plant them and take care of them as they sprout and grow. Then she quickly reminded me of the story of Jack and the Beanstalk that she had read to me earlier.

The next summer I too had hollyhocks in all of their brilliant colors blooming along our yard fence. And just like Miss Ella's, they appeared in "Technicolor" and drew the most discriminating eye in awe and admiration. More than 65 years have passed, but my childhood curiosity never dulled. A year or so ago, I returned for a respectful visit to the remains of what once had been the little white house with the rusty tin roof. Not much remained of the house and barn: just piles of rotting wood, the stone steps to what had been the front porch, a few scattered pieces of tin, the stone fireplace chimney...and Miss Ella's hollyhocks blooming everywhere in dazzling, radiant, colorful profusion. It's funny, but I swear they remembered me, tilting their flower heads in my direction and giving me a reassuring nod and gentle wave. Of course, it could have been the gentle summer breeze.

END

CHRISTMAS MORNING 1943

It was early morning, the 25th day of December 1943, and cold, really cold. A heavy blanket of sparkling white snow covered everything for miles around. Strong gusts of wind had swirled the snow into high drifts against our fencerows and covered the fence posts in spots. Everything seemed to glisten. For the past several days the temperature hovered near zero. Long dazzling icicles reached from the eaves of the old, weathered gray, two-story farmhouse, and some even stretched their long icy spears all the way to the frozen snow that lay on the ground.

The springs of the old double bed squeaked and groaned irritably as my mother turned over and rolled out of bed, her feet hitting the cold linoleum floor. It was 4:00 a.m., the same time she rose every morning, all year round. In the blue-black of predawn, her hands knowingly found the familiar spot on the mantel where the box of Diamond brand wood matches always rested. The match head sparked to a bright flame as she gave it a quick drag across the sandpaper strip on the side of the box followed by a swift snap of her wrist. The familiar scratching, crackling, and popping sounds of the match were somehow comforting in the cold darkness, serving up a promise that the room would soon be warm. Lifting the globe from the old coal oil lamp, she touched the match to the wick, and with practiced fingers made slight adjustments to produce a bright yellow flame. Replacing the globe, and bathed in the warm glow of the lamp, she turned her attention to the ashes and hot coals in the stone fireplace.

She was careful to not let her long outing gown get too close. The iron shovel and poker scraped metal against stone as she shoveled away the covering of ashes, exposing red coals left over from the roaring fire of the night before. She added kindling, then seasoned split hickory logs, making sure the kindling was burning steadily. Fire blazing, she hastily returned to the warmth of homemade quilts and the big feather bed that she and Dad shared.

Awake, I quietly watched the bright flames through the bars of my baby bed as they grew to warm the room and cast long shadows on the wallpapered walls. Mother and Dad were talking in low tones about the coming events of the day, while my anticipation grew faster than the flames. This was the magic day! It was finally here. Christmas—the first one that I can really remember. I was so excited that I could hardly contain myself. I couldn't wait to see what "Santy Claus" had delivered. I had worried for weeks, although it seemed like a lifetime, about how the man in the red suit would manage to maneuver his rather rotund self and his giant bag of treats and toys down our chimney.

Mother and Dad had both been talking about "Old Santy" for weeks, acting rather mysteriously and secretive. Passing knowing looks, they whispered a lot when I was around, and they kept asking me questions about what I wanted for Christmas. Like most parents, they reminded me throughout the year to "be good or "Santy Claus" won't come to our house." They scared the pants off me with warnings of how "Old Santy" would "scratch my eyes out" if I wasn't asleep when he came down the chimney.

Now, finally after what must have seemed to them like hours of "Can I get up now" and "Is it Christmas yet??" my mother finally got out of bed. She came and lifted me over the wood railing of the baby bed, with a happy-as-sunshine "Let's see what "Santy Claus" brought you last night." Dad climbed out of bed, slipped his overalls on over his long-handled drawers, and reached for the iron poker. He punched at the brightly burning logs, sending sparks showering up the chimney. I thought that was neat, and I couldn't wait until I was old enough to poke the logs and make them spark like my dad did.

World War II was raging. Times were awfully hard, and there was very little cash money in 1943, but somehow "Santy Claus" managed to bring a couple of oranges and apples, bags of red grapes, raisins, nuts and chocolate drops along with sugar-coated orange slice candy. All were rare treats, seldom seen except at Christmas. And there, next to the fireplace, was the most wonderful gift of all, my very own little red wooden rocking chair.

I promptly parked myself in the chair with all my other wonderful Christmas goodies in my lap and on the floor at my feet. "Billy, you can have a piece or two of candy, and a few grapes, but don't eat any more until after breakfast," Mother said as she headed for the kitchen to start breakfast. I sat and rocked in that chair, proud as a peacock, until breakfast was ready. I savored my treats, daydreamed about the rest of the day ahead of me, and pondered how in the world "Santy Claus" made his way down that chimney without me hearing him. Dad, now fully dressed in his heavy denim coat and winter cap with earflaps down, was out the door and to the barn to milk the cows and feed the livestock, his mind set on his mission, and as usual, a man of very few words even during the holidays.

That little rocker was one of the first things that I could claim as all mine. Year 'round, I would sit in it and rock for hours at a time as my mother read me stories of the Three Little Pigs and Goldilocks and the Three Bears. At night when we listened to the old cathedral, battery-powered RCA Victor radio, I prudently positioned myself in my rocker near the radio and anxiously awaited the airing of our favorite programs. My chair and I had our own special spot in front of the fireplace. I still have that little red chair, and it rocks quietly in a place of prominence in our home. But that Christmas morning long ago, I sat for a long while in front of that fire bewildered by, and a bit fearful of, this magical, marvelous "Santy Claus" who came down the chimney toting a bag filled with candy and toys for kids who had been especially good. A man who brought such wonder and joy, but would wreak havoc if you were bad or if you were awake and saw him making his rounds.

The world was a white winter wonderland as far as the eye could see. The morning was clear and still, and the bright sun turned the snow into a dreamland studded with sparkling diamonds of frost. After breakfast, and with the chores all done, we bundled up to head across the fields the couple of miles, as a crow flies, to Pa and Ma's house. Down the path by our barn, past the big old sycamore tree at the head of the spring, along the fencerow that was a guide to our way east, and across the fields to my grandparents' farm. Mother had placed the few brightly wrapped and ribboned Christmas gifts in brown paper grocery sacks that she and Dad each now carried. Mother's family was gathering for Christmas dinner, and the snow was too deep and dangerous for our old Model A Ford to make the trip around the road. Dad led the way, Mother followed, and I came behind, lifting my short 4-year-old legs high to try to clear the snow as I stepped in their tracks. It didn't take long for me to tire out, so Dad hoisted me to his shoulders, and there I rode for the rest of the trip. We passed by the old holly tree at the edge of our neighbor, Bill Short's woodlot, the holly berries and leaves peeking bright red and green from under the heavy mantle of snow. A cardinal couple added to the color and spent their Christmas morning pecking at the berries.

I was so cold that I thought I would freeze to death before I finally spotted curling smoke from Pa and Ma's chimney in the distance. I forgot all about being cold as we reached the top of the hill above their house, and my anticipation and excitement began to surge again. Then, it was down the hill and past the chicken brooder, smokehouse and garage. After removing our overshoes on the front porch, and knocking the loose snow from our clothes, we joined the smiles and laughter as we stepped through the door of the old whitewashed board-and-batten house and greeted everyone with hugs, presents and homemade treats.

From the moment we hit the threshold, my senses were overcome with the magnificent aromas and happiness wafting through the house. It was as if I had stepped onto a carousel, a whirlwind of desserts baking, country ham, vegetables, dried apples, spices and peaches all mingled with wood smoke from the fireplace and Dad and Pa's pipe tobacco. Add to that the thick and wonderful smell of cedar hovering throughout the house from the Christmas tree that Ma had decorated with strings of popcorn, chains made of colored poster paper and Christmas cards of past years. There was the pleasant musical hum of conversation from the women as they prepared dinner in the kitchen and gossiped about the neighbors, while the men gathered around the fireplace in the living room, smoked their pipes and talked of spring planting and whether their supply of hay and corn was going to be enough to feed the stock through the winter.

Times were particularly tough with the war going on, and the adult gift exchange consisted mostly of utility gifts such as a Pyrex bowl or a tube of Pepsodent toothpaste and a toothbrush, hand-embroidered pillowcases and tablecloths or something crocheted. The men got socks or handkerchiefs, pipe tobacco or a couple of packs of cigarettes. There simply wasn't money available to spend on Christmas gifts, and everyone was thankful for what they received.

My cousins, Pat, Dixie, Buck and Larry shared their toys, and we played all afternoon with whirligigs, yo-yos, a musical spinning top and a wooden droopy hound pull-toy with floppy ears. We ate sticks of peppermint and pillows of brightly striped Christmas candy, hard enough to break our teeth, and apples, oranges and grapes. We sneaked into the dining room to pilfer sample bites of chicken and ham from the platters on the table, only to get caught and fussed at by our grandmother, Ma. It's a miracle that we all didn't get a bad tummy ache, but if we did, I don't remember it.

Christmas dinner was the time that the women folk showed off their cooking expertise. There was enough good country cooking spread across the dining table that day to cause the legs to buckle. There was country ham, chicken n' dumplins, dressing and gravy, sausage, roast beef, pinto beans, green beans, mashed potatoes, and fried corn. There were biscuits, light bread, and corn muffins, served with molasses, jams, jellies, and preserves, and homemade sweet cream hand-churned butter. The desserts were scrumptious, a mouth-watering assortment that included coconut cake, chocolate cake with white icing, pineapple upside-down cake and fruit cake. There were apple and peach cobblers, chocolate and caramel pies, fried peach pies and banana pudding. And if that wasn't enough, there was homemade vanilla ice cream in aluminum ice trays in the refrigerator. I favored the pineapple upside-down cake, although I made every attempt to sample them all.

Going home that night, I once again hitched a ride on Dad's shoulders. The moon on the snow made the night bright as day, and I was cold...really cold. In spite of the cold, there was a warm glow of remembrance of all the day's joy and goodness as we crunched through the snow and the night wind swirled around us. I relived that day on top of Dad's shoulders, moment by moment, all of the fun, the good food, and the excitement that we had shared, and the trip home seemed to be so very short. I wished with all my might that day would never end.

END

THE LITTLE CHURCH ON FUSS HOLLER ROAD

It was a beautiful Sunday morning. Everything outdoors was fresh and smelled clean—washed by a passing spring thundershower the night before. It was mid-March, 1944, and I was spending the weekend with my grandparents as I did several times a year.

My grandmother, "Ma," had called me for breakfast for the third time. Finally, the morning sun's rays spilling through the white lace curtains of the guest room window plus the lingering sound and smell of country sausage frying in the skillet forced me out from under the pile of homemade quilts. I had spent the night in Ma's guest room with its slightly musty smell and big featherbed.

I quickly slipped into my much patched and faded "worn-out" overalls and a short-sleeved shirt. I pulled on my socks and my old scuffed-up leather work shoes. Dressed, I ran to the dining room to find a warm plate of fried eggs, sausage and biscuits. A bowl of sawmill gravy sat next to the plate, along with one of Ma's cut-glass goblets filled with fresh milk. In addition, Ma had placed a bowl of Post Toasties on the table to which she had added cut-up wild strawberries and sprinkled on sugar, just enough to make the bowl's contents sparkle. Soon as I finished the plate of sausage, eggs and gravy-covered biscuits, I was ready for the bowl of cereal. After all, I was a growing boy and had a "bottomless pit," according to Ma.

I covered the toasted flakes with fresh milk that I poured from the glass jug that Ma had placed on the table next to my cereal bowl. I seldom ever got Post Toasties for breakfast at home, so I took my time, relishing every sweet crunchy bite of this special treat. While I finished stuffing myself with Ma's wonderful breakfast, she said, "Take your time eating your Post Toasties, but soon as you're through, you can help me pour grape juice into the church communion glasses. This is the third Sunday in the month, Communion Sunday," Ma continued as she busied herself in the kitchen, drying and storing the dishes from her and my grandfather, "Pa's," breakfast. They both were up before daylight and had eaten their breakfast hours ago.

Welch's Grape Juice was a substitute for the church wine that the little congregation couldn't afford on their limited budget, and besides, they weren't too sure about drinking wine in the church house, anyway.

The trays for the communion glasses were made entirely of silver plate. Each tray was round, maybe 18 inches in diameter, and the trays were double-stacked so the combined height was about 6 inches. The communion glasses were small, of clear crystal and a size comparable to a shot glass, if you'll forgive the comparison. The holes in the trays held 60 or more glasses. The cover of the tray had a centered, upright cross.

Ma got the quart bottle of Welch's Grape Juice down from its place on the top shelf of her kitchen cupboard, unscrewed the top and carefully filled each small glass with an exact amount of the sweet, purple liquid. My job was to place each glass in the holes that would keep them from sliding around and spilling. "Be real careful and try not to spill any, because if you do, then we'll have to empty the entire tray, wash it and start all over again," Ma said. I wasn't real excited about starting over, so I tried extra hard and managed not to spill any of the juice.

A box of unleavened bread (it looked a lot like regular crackers to me) was already on the table, and we broke several of them into tiny pieces, enough to cover the bottoms of two smaller, and matching, silver-plated trays with lids. In about 30 minutes, our job of filling glasses and "breaking bread" was completed, but it sure seemed to me that it took a lot longer.

"Ma, how come church folks drink grape juice and eat crackers on communion Sunday?"

A smile slowly spread across her face, then she became serious. "Why child, the wine symbolizes the blood of Christ that was shed on the cross for all the world's sins, and the broken bread symbolizes his broken body."

"Ma, what does symbolism mean?"

"Mercy child, you're just full of questions. Listen to what the preacher talks about today. Then I'll read you about the Lord's last supper from the Bible, and after that, I'll try to explain what symbolism means."

Ma looked at the clock on the nightstand next to her and Pa's bed, which was visible through the door of the dining room where we had been loading the trays. She exclaimed, "Mercy me, look at the time, Billy Boy, it's almost 8 o'clock. We have to hurry, or we're going to be late for church."

Hurrying to the kitchen and to the washstand in the corner, I filled the white enamel wash pan half full of hot water from the kettle on the stove. The water had been heating all morning on Ma's old wood-burning kitchen range. There was no bathroom in my grandparents' home; in fact, there was no running water or indoor plumbing. Their source of water for the household cooking and bathing was a spring that was 50 yards or more away from their house. At least twice a day, we made trips to the spring to fill two white enamel water buckets to carry back to the house. I tagged along with Pa when he made trips to the spring and had my own 1 gallon, metal "syrup bucket" to do my share of fetching water.

Pa and Ma lived on a small farm a quarter mile off the main road, and since they had no close neighbors, there were no bathing privacy issues. In the warm summer months, Pa was known to occasionally bathe in one of Ma's washtubs in the shade of a big pecan tree in their backyard. On this particular Sunday morning, I took the pan of hot water, a washcloth, towel and a small piece of Ma's homemade lye soap to the relative privacy of their small screened-in porch at the back of the house. I stripped down to my drawers, gave myself a "wash-pan" bath and towel dried. I put on my best "go to church" clothes: a white short-sleeve shirt, blue striped seersucker pants held up with blue, clip-on suspenders, blue socks and polished, brown "Red Goose" shoes. Ma had a small round mirror on a metal stand that I used to see how to wet-comb my fine, wispy blond hair. Combing my hair was at best a temporary measure, for in a few minutes, it would be dry and down in my eyes again.

The mirror was two-sided; one side had a normal view, and the other, a magnified view. I thought the magnified view was just too cool, and I had fun looking at my "big eye." I turned my head sideways so I could see an enlarged profile of my nose in the mirror, which once again convinced me that it was way too large and terribly misshapen.

While I was taking my bath, Pa was in the keeping room, preparing to shave a week's growth of white beard stubble. Try as she might, Ma couldn't get Pa to shave more than once a week, unless there was a funeral of a neighbor or family member that he was obliged to attend out of common decency. A small round mirror at his eye level hung on a nail just above the small door to the storage area that was beneath the narrow stairs to the attic. The stairs were in the corner of the keeping room near the fireplace, and Pa used the area underneath the stairs to store his shaving stuff and his barber tools. Pa was a "sometimes" country barber and would cut his neighbors' hair on occasion for a little extra income.

This morning he sharpened his straight razor, slapping out a rhythm on the leather razor strap, until the degree of sharpness met with his test thumb's approval. Applying a wet shaving brush to the soap in the shaving cup, Pa vigorously stirred the soap into a frothy lather that he applied to his beard. Then, with the dexterity of a surgeon, he shaved off the week's growth of stubble. A couple of tiny, but bloody, nicks were covered with small pieces of "roll-your-own" cigarette paper that he would carefully remove just before entering the church house. The small white pieces of paper gave Pa's face sort of a *patched together* look.

I'm in awe of those men, including my dad and granddad that had the courage to shave with a straight razor, which I consider a lethal weapon. I would watch as they shaved, avoiding earlobes, noses and Adam's apples. I never had the courage to try to use a straight razor. I chose instead to use a safety razor. Thank goodness, as I would have probably lobbed off an ear or worse with a straight razor.

Clean-shaven and "wash-pan" scrubbed clean, Pa got dressed in his only Sunday clothes: a brown pinstripe suit, white shirt slightly frayed at the collar and cuffs, out-of-style conservative tie, black socks and polished, but well-worn, brown shoes. He had worn that suit every Sunday for at least 15 years.

Ma, well-scrubbed from her bath the Saturday night before, was powdered, rouged and hair arranged in a bun. She was dressed in her prettiest homemade Sunday dress, the one with the tiny red rose pattern all over, and white collar trimmed in lace. On her feet were her sensible black laced shoes (no spiked heels for Ma). With all the scrubbing, shaving, combing and dressing complete, we were out the back kitchen door by 8:45 that morning. Ma had inspected my ears to be sure that they were clean. Then she predictably spit on her handkerchief for the additional reaming out of my ears. No matter how hard I tried, I could never seem to get my ears clean enough by my own hand to not be "spit washed" by my grandmother.

As we left the house, Pa was carrying his big, thick, black leather Bible and a frayed songbook with the back cover missing.

Ma had the short straps of her plain black leather purse in one hand and was balancing the big silver communion tray with the other. I was carrying the smaller silver "cracker" trays and my Sunday school book.

To reach the garage, where Pa parked his 1931 A-Model, we took the path across the yard, still muddy from the rain of the night before, tiptoeing carefully, trying our best to keep the mud off our Sunday shoes. Pa settled in the driver's seat, turned the key in the ignition and pressed the foot starter button in the floor-board. After a few growling turns, the starter caught, and the old car shook as the engine grumbled to life, with the exhaust puffing blue smoke. Pa backed the car slowly out of the garage, giving any cats or chickens roosting underneath an opportunity to make a squawking, feathers-flying escape. Ma and I climbed in the car and got settled, me in the back seat with the "cracker" trays, and Ma sitting next to Pa with the communion tray and black imitation leather purse in her lap. Pa drove the car slowly down the muddy lane toward the main road. The lane to Pa's house always seemed to be rutted and washed out. He was forever shoveling, and filling ruts with dirt and rocks. The ruts caused the old car to bounce around like a bucking bronco. I now wonder how Ma kept from spilling every drop of that precious communion "wine." The main "Fuss Holler" road that led to Gregory's Chapel Cumberland Presbyterian Church was less than a mile from my grandparents' house. The county road had gained its infamous moniker years before because the entire community always seemed to be in a fuss and uproar. My grandparents hated the name "fuss holler," preferring to call the road by its official name, the Albright Hollow Road. My granddad didn't help matters any, as for years he patrolled the perimeter of his farm with a loaded 22, making sure a neighbor, Tom Holt, an adjoining farmer, never set foot on his property. I was never sure what that feud was all about; some-thing about a property fence line I've been told. I do know that Pa was set to shoot first and ask questions later, and so was Mr. Holt, but fortunately no shots were ever fired by either party.

The gravel county road was rutted and filled with a lot of large mud holes. We bounced along, the car's back wheels slinging mud, spinning and sliding all the way to the lane turnoff that led up the hill to the grounds of the church house.

As we turned off the main road and climbed a few feet up the lane that led to the church; the car stopped, getting stuck in gummy, wet, red clay mud. Cars that climbed the hill before us had left axle-deep ruts in the lane. The back wheels of Pa's old car kept spinning and spinning until it was buried up to the frame and axle. The car wasn't moving an inch, so Ma, showing a little disgust, opened her car door and climbed out with a mind to walk through the mud up the hill to the church house, carrying her purse and the communion tray, which she did. Pa and I started working to get the car unstuck. He put me under the steering wheel where I had to stretch my short legs to reach the clutch and the accelerator, or foot feed as we called it. "Give it the gas, son, while I try to push us out," Pa said, as he heaved and grunted and pushed the old car until he was almost out of breath. The car didn't budge an inch, and the only thing that we succeeded in doing was spattering Pa's suit from top to bottom with mud from the spinning tires.

Finally, seeing our plight, several men who were already at the church came to our aid, and all pushing at the same time, finally pushed the car out of the mud hole. They continued pushing the car up the hill until at last, the car, Pa, me and our rescuers all covered in varying degrees of mud spatters, reached the gravel parking area directly in front of the church. We were all a muddy, sorry-looking sight when we walked into the church, leaving a trail of mud from our shoes. That didn't seem to dampen anyone's spirits, and we settled into the morning church services anyway, mud and all.

The Gregory's Chapel Cumberland Presbyterian Church, which sat atop a small grassy knoll, was surrounded on the back and both sides by woods. The church was small, of white clapboard, with no steeple or bell. Two separate doors were in the front, one for the men to enter and one for the women, a holdover from the days when the men and women sat separately. To a small degree, they were still segregated, although most families sat together. The church interior was as simple as the outside. The walls and ceiling were covered in bead board, painted white, and the floors were of varnished oak.

There was no electricity in the little church, but two rows of kerosene lamps were suspended by chains from the ceiling. The lamps didn't supply much light, but on cloudy Sundays and during the "Big Meetings" held at night, they were filled with kerosene and lit. I suppose they were better than no light at all, but barely. The thing that I remember most was the hundreds of flying insects that they drew on summer nights, keeping everyone busy slapping at the critters. At the front of the church stood a small stage with a podium. Two fancy, carved chairs with burgundy velvet seat covers sat against the wall directly behind the podium, provided a place for the preacher to sit.

Again reflecting the historical segregation of men and women in the church, two rows of uncomfortable wooden pews divided by an aisle went down the center of the church.

Near the front of the church and off to one side was a small wood-burning cast-iron heater that had been fired up to knock off some of the chill of the still cool early spring. A small stack of split hickory wood was stacked next to the stove. In spite of the stove, the inside of the church always seemed to be cold, fall, winter and spring. In the summer it was sweating hot even with all the windows open and the hand-powered cardboard fans going full speed.

The church had a small, but constant and faithful membership. Almost all were families living on small farms up and down Fuss

Hollow Road. Most had little monetary income, and they couldn't afford to purchase a piano or pump organ, so they sang a cappella. Pa was the song leader and had to set the pitch by humming (it sounded like a painful grunt to me, at the time). He led each song in his mumbling gravel voice. Pa was a terrible singer, but you had to give him credit for the effort he put forth. In spite of Pa's singing, the songs and the singing sounded good to my young ears. These were songs that had been sung in Southern Protestant churches for 150 years or more. I can still hear the strains of "Shall We Gather at the River," "Amazing Grace" and "The Little Brown Church in the Wildwood."

After a few songs and a prayer, we went to our respective Sunday school classes. Each class gathered in a section of the open church sanctuary, and with every class talking at the same time, it could get really noisy and confusing. My Sunday school teacher was Miss Estelle Scott, a slightly plump, stern spinster with a corset that was too tight. She talked to us about Jesus and how he loved little children, but would discipline us severely if we were not really good little boys and girls. And if we were bad and didn't obey our parents, He would send us to a really hot place some day. My Sunday school book had a color picture on the front of Jesus holding a baby lamb with a lot of sheep surrounding him. I thought how he looked really kind, and I wondered if he could possibly be as mean as my teacher said he was. I was always happy when Sunday school was over, because Ms. Scott always made me feel uncomfortable and embarrassed by asking me questions from the Bible that I couldn't answer, or she would want us to quote Bible verses that I could never seem to remember.

The preacher, who Pa referred to as "Old Brother Brown," when he wasn't around, was a barrel-chested bull of a man, standing 6 foot 6 and equipped with a thundering voice. Every Sunday, he roared hellfire, brimstone and damnation as he pounded the podium when he stood on that little stage. Sometimes I would fall asleep during the sermon, my head on Ma's lap only to jump straight up, awakened by his hollering and pounding extra loud to make a point. His preaching scared the dickens out of me and put the fear of God into the most wayward spirit in the congregation. Some allowed that he was always preaching directly at them. I guess they must have had a guilty conscience.

I loved the congregation's singing, but my short attention span was quickly bored with the preaching no matter how energetic and loud it was. And though the message was usually simple, I really didn't understand most of it, so I dozed or gazed at the outside world through windows that lined both sides of the church. The sun was shining. Everything was starting to turn that soft green that you only see in the early spring. An abundance of redbud and white dogwood trees filled the surrounding woods with blossoms in all their profusion. Cardinal, bluebird and robin couples scolded or sang as they flew from limb to limb. Several birds hopped through the grass looking for bugs and worms while selecting and pulling perfect blades of grass to add to the nests they were building.

Occasionally, I would start to nod off, and Ma would gently elbow me in the ribs, or she would lean over to whisper, "pay attention, this is important," in my ear. Finally, after what seemed an eternity of squirming in my seat, dozing and staring out the window; the collection plates were passed around, and folks added as much as they could afford. There was the soft rustle of checks, folding money and the clink of coins as they dropped into the bowl. My grandparents believed in tithing and faithfully gave 10 percent of their small annual income. I don't know that tithing ever created any appreciable hardship in their lives, but if it did, they never let on.

After the sermon, Pa led a few more songs. Then finally, at last, the communion trays were passed, and each member selected one of the tiny glasses and a small, broken piece of bread I wasn't offered either of these as "I wasn't a church member yet," Ma said. The preacher said a few words, the meaning that I didn't really understand. Then everyone drank from the little glasses at the same time. The preacher said a few more words. Everyone put the broken piece of bread in their mouths. The preacher said another prayer. At last, the communion services were completed, and the invitation was given, but no one responded. Pa selected the final song from the hymnbook, mumbled and growled his way through. The preacher rattled the rafters with his closing prayer, asking God to have mercy on all the lost sinners and this Sunday's "church" drew to a close.

I was near starved to death, but nearly everyone, including my grandparents, stayed around for a half-hour or more after church services to visit with the preacher and the neighbors. There were discussions of the morning's sermon, and neighbors had to catch up on any community gossip that they might have missed from the previous week's eavesdropping on the telephone party line.

Ma gathered together a small group of ladies to discuss sending money and canned fruit and vegetables to the Monroe Harding Children's Home in Nashville, an orphanage that was supported in part by the Cumberland Presbyterian churches.

Finally, just as I was almost passing out from hunger, we climbed into the old A-Model for the slipping, sliding and mud-slinging trip back down the muddy Fuss Hollow Road to Pa and Ma's house. I could hardly wait to taste the fried chicken dinner that Ma had prepared early that morning, long before I crawled out of bed.

The preacher was dedicated to saving souls that Sunday morning. My dedication was surviving starvation long enough to get home to Ma's fried chicken, sweet tea and homemade coconut cake.

END

THE WATER JUG ANTHOLOGY

One lonely buttercup stood proudly as if still among the many that once guarded the edges of what had been our driveway. I carefully wheeled my truck in and parked where traces of creek gravel peeked through scraggly weeds and grass that hid much of the driveway's definition.

My family had sharecropped this old farm when I was 13. The property, long ago willed by the previous owners to the local Presbyterian Church, had been sadly neglected. Familiar buildings had fallen down. The barn and tractor shed no longer existed, replaced with weeds and wild rose vines. Except for the hand-chiseled limestone chimney and front steps nestled in overgrowth, the old two-story house, where we had lived, was nothing more than a ghost and a small pile of rotting lumber and bent, rusting tin.

But time had smiled on the old toolshed, and though it sagged slightly, it still stood defiant against time and nature's elements. A wooden latch still held the large front door to the building in place. Sliding the latch back, I gave the door a slight lift and a hard pull. Grudgingly, the old door swung on its rusty hinges. The door hadn't been opened in years and the bottom dragged rebelliously against the accumulated dirt and tall grass that grew along its edges. I managed to pry open the door just enough to squeeze through. Sunlight shone through cracks between the boards that formed the walls of the old building, becoming golden rays through the dust that I stirred up. The shed seemed to be mostly empty except for a few old, rusty farm tools and abandoned, unidentifiable machine parts. A couple of Nehi Grape bottles sat on a wall plate, and were older than me. A thick layer of dust covered the bottles and everything else in the shed.

Nothing here for me, I thought to myself as I took one last departing look around the old shed's interior before squeezing back through the door to the outside world. Something suddenly caught my eye…a flash, a glint of sunlight on glass. Sitting alone on a shelf was an old glass gallon jug wrapped in rotting burlap. The burlap or what remained of it was held in place with hemp baler twine. I like to believe a bit of magic was afoot that day as just enough of the glass was showing through the dust for the sun to set off a sparkle. Finding an old glass water jug wouldn't be very exciting to most folks, but this was "our" water jug, my Dad's and mine.

It had never been much to look at: just an old glass jar with a zinc screw-on top. The jar once held a gallon of apple cider vinegar or perhaps cucumber pickles. The burlap wrapping had once been a Purina hog feed sack. As a finishing touch, a leather thong was looped around the neck of the jug. The thong was used for carrying. How we welcomed the sight of it when it was filled with cool water from the springhouse, or the well. We soaked the burlap to keep the water cool for delivery to a throat-parched farmer in the dusty fields of July and August.

Memories flooded over me…summer days of hard work, dust, sweat, blisters, hay bales, honeysuckle, sun-browned skin, bare feet, swimming holes and cool spring water. With a bit of a lump in my throat and my eyes slightly misty, I gently took the old jug down from the shelf, careful not to lose the burlap wrapping and carefully squeezed through the door. Placing the old jug in the seat bedside me, I turned the ignition, started the truck and eased slowly down the driveway and back 60 years in time… to a peaceful existence, gentle thoughts and maybe a little bit of innocence. Times gone by and memories to recapture with my old water jug.

THE WATER JUG & SPRING PLOWING

The hinges squeaked and groaned painfully, stiff with rust and time. I need to bring the oilcan the next time I come to the field, I thought to myself as I pulled and tugged. The bottom corner of the old wooden gate dragged deep curving grooves in the powdery dust formed by a too-dry spring. My big black shepherd dog, Joe, and I pushed and squirmed our way through the narrow opening between the gate and the gatepost. It had taken most of my runt, 9-year-old strength to open the big gate, gone gray and wrinkled from years of weathering hot summers and cold winters. It blocked the entrance to the 20-acre field where long rows of young cornstalks, no more than 6 inches tall, glistened bright green. Dew drops sparkling like jewels in the early morning sun clung to the tips of the leaves and to lacy spider webs that were anchored to the tiny stalks and the few scattered weeds.

I had just come from the springhouse where I had filled up the glass water jug and wet down the burlap wrapping, then lingered for a while, as 9-year-old boys are prone to do. The old stone springhouse, which was several yards behind our stock barn, squatted solidly at the base of a 50-foot sheer limestone bluff. The bluff formed the edge of an old-growth woods of walnut, hickory and oak. It was always pleasantly cool and damp at the springhouse, even in the stagnant heat of the dog days of summer. Lichen and a layer of thick green moss covered the weathered wood shingle roof. The walls were of hand-chiseled limestone, the solid work of slaves, and one open window in the side let the light in. A doorway in front gave access to the cool, dark interior; if a door ever existed, it was no more. The frames and sills were partially rotted away. Instead of a floor, a walkway around the sides surrounded a shallow pool of cool spring water, no more than 18-inches deep. A half-gallon jug that once had held Karo Syrup and now held milk was resting up to its neck in the pool staying cool for our supper. The spring was a magical spot for a kid, a place of imaginary elves and fairies. I had stayed too long, way too long daydreaming and enjoying the moist coolness and the fresh smells of damp moss and wild mint. I looked for bull-frogs that lay hidden under the watercress with only their bulging eyes above the water and saw none. I became oblivious of time as I tried in vain to catch a member of the school of silverside minnows as they darted to and fro over the smooth brown gravel. The gravel covered the bottom of the shallow, crystal-clear pool inside the springhouse.

Finally, I looked up at the sun, and a shiver of panic ran up my spine, as I realized that by now Dad would be dirt-parched thirsty and most likely irritated to the point of tanning my hide.

Now, through the gate, I absently stuck my forefinger through the hole where a bent rusty nail had snagged the bib of my thread-bare overalls, ripping yet another place in the pocket. Joe wiggled and squirmed his way through the gate at my heel. As the heat of the morning sun burned through his long, glossy black coat; his pink tongue lolled out the side of his mouth. Hassling, he looked up at me, his eyes bright, expectant and his ears standing at attention. His four white-and-brown feet danced to the excitement of this early morning adventure. To Joe, everything was an adventure.

Dust squished tiny mushroom clouds between my bare toes, and as I walked, I carefully protected the burlap-wrapped water jug. The wet burlap provided insulation and evaporation that kept the water cool.

Overgrown locust scrub, wild plum bushes and blackberry briars mixed with tall brown grass, a remnant from the previous winter, lined the fencerows that surrounded the field. Making snorting sounds of expectation, Joe nosed around the grass until he jump-started a startled rabbit that led the big shepherd in an erratic zigzag chase down the fencerow. Walking along the edge of the field for a dozen yards I changed course and started across the freshly cultivated ground, careful not to step on the small stalks of corn. I walked toward the moving dust cloud in the distance that was my father driving the old green-and-yellow John Deere "B" tractor. The freshly cultivated earth felt cool to my bare feet, and the pleasantly warm "earthy" smell filled my nostrils. I kept my eyes glued to the ground, as usual, looking for "Indian money," arrowheads, stone axes and other prehistoric stone treasures to add to my cigar box collection. My concentration was such that I didn't see the big black racer snake until I was almost on top if it. With a "whoop," I cleared the snake and a good section of cornfield. Joe came bounding and commenced barking, snapping and running a tight circle around the snake. The big racer made a couple of half-hearted pretend strikes at Joe before slipping away into the protection of the tall grass and weeds along the edge of the field. Joe leapfrogged after the snake for a bit before losing interest. The adrenalin still surging and my heart pounding from the snake encounter, I started paying a darn sight more attention to where I planted my bare feet as I continued toward the billowing cloud of dust moving in the distance.

As I got close, Dad pulled the hand clutch stick back, bringing the old tractor to an abrupt halt. The loud, familiar "chuka, chuka chuka" of the two-cylinder engine calmed to a quieter "put...put... pop, pop, pop" as he eased back on the throttle.

The sound of the John Deere tractor was music to his ears, and to mine, as the spinning flywheel hummed and the pleasant smells of tractor fuel mixed with warm grease and field dust filled the air.

He tipped the old pith "safari" helmet he was wearing down in front so that the visor shielded his eyes from the bright mid-morning sun. Dust emphasized deep lines creasing his face and neck, the exposed skin tanned to rich leather. His eyes had a perpetual squint from too many days in the sun. He stood up, stretched, then, using the steel frame of the cultivator as a step, eased his lanky 6' 2" frame off the tractor and to the ground in one fluid motion.

He reached for the water jug, and with both hands, lifted and drank long and deep. Water overflowed from the corners of his mouth, making tiny rivers through the field dust that covered his face and neck, then running down to stain the front of his shirt dark.

Passing the jug back to me, he tilted the helmet back on his head as he wiped the dirt and sweat from his face with his faded blue bandana handkerchief.

"I saw you coming across the field; what did you and Joe roust up?" he asked.

"Just a big ole black racer," I replied, feeling brave and important.

"Joe kill it?" he asked.

"Nope, just chased it into the weeds in the fencerow close to the gate." I said.

"Good, they help keep the field mouse population down. "Didn't come after you; did he? I heard old folks talk about seeing black racers chasing people, particularly 9-year-old barefoot boys."

He paused then and looking me straight in the eye, said seriously, "Son, the next time you take this long to bring me a drink of water, I'm going to bust your hide. You're about 2 hours late, and I was just about parched and spitting cotton. You understand me, son?" I looked down at my feet, kicking at a clod with my bare big toe, I nodded "yes sir," as I knew that he meant every word.

Reaching for the gold chain attached to the bib of his overalls, he carefully pulled the small gold and silver engraved pocket watch from its special pocket. He snapped open the cover, and he duly noted the time. Looking up at the whereabouts of the sun, he said, "Now, go on back to the house and tell your mother that I'll finish plowing this patch of ground before I come to dinner.

Should be there in another hour or so. Leave the jug over there in the fencerow. It'll stay cool in the shade of that big walnut tree.

In a single move he was back in the iron tractor seat, pushing the throttle lever open with one hand as he engaged the hand clutch in one fluid motion. The old tractor grudgingly popped and snorted a few puffs of black smoke from the smokestack as Dad pointed the tractor's front end down the long, straight corn rows toward the far side of the field. The earth-polished, silver points of the cultivator were tilling the rich brown earth, all giving anticipation of tall green cornstalks with big yellow ears of Neal's Paymaster to be picked in the fall. Joe and I headed back toward the house with more unknown adventures lying in wait around every turn in the path.

THE WATER JUG & THE GRAIN BINDER

It was 7:30 a.m. The sun was already a scorcher, burning a brilliant white circle out of the blue sky on that late July day in 1948. If a breeze was stirring anywhere you couldn't tell it for not a leaf moved. His faded tan twill shirt was salt-streaked and sweat-soaked.

He was all over the old grain binder, crawling under and reaching into the guts of the machine, using the hand-pump grease gun and freshly filled squirt oil can. He seemed intent on greasing or oiling every spot on the old machine that might have a bit of friction or movement. Kate and Polly, the big bay and white Percheron horses, were enjoying the quiet moment before their work began, heads down, eyes closed, occasionally snorting and shaking their heads at the ever-present gnats that buzzed around their eyes and noses. Polly stamped her hooves irritably as an overly aggressive horsefly got carried away as it shopped for lunch.

Occasionally, the horses shifted their heavy leather harnesses for just a bit more comfort.

From somewhere under the binder, Dad's voice came, "Son, I forgot my ball-peen hammer, and I need it and those two open-end wrenches that I mostly keep in the binder toolbox. I forgot to bring them with me this morning. They should be on top when you open the gray metal toolbox in back of the garage. You might as well go and get 'em as I'll most likely need them before this morning is over. While you're at it, bring us back a jug of fresh water from the spring. Don't forget to wet down the burlap good so the water in the jug will stay cool. Go on now and don't stop and look at every bug and rock along the way, or you won't be back here before suppertime. And don't try to catch every minnow in the spring branch, either. While you're at it, run by the house and ask your Mother what we're having for dinner. I feel like one of her caramel pies, if she's in a baking mood. Now go on and mind me about foolin' along and wastin' too much time."

With that said, he hoisted himself into the old iron seat high up and at the back part of the binder. The seat was positioned so the driver could handle the team of horses or mules and watch all the binder's moving parts at the same time, just in case there was one of the all too-frequent breakdowns. Binders were known to break down frequently because of all the moving parts. He gently shook the reins, clucked words of encouragement to the team of big horses as he adjusted each of the three hand levers that were about knee level in front of him. The team moved out, and the old binder lurched, grumbled and clattered noisily to life.

The old McCormick binder was a rusty relic, but it worked with the precision of a Swiss timepiece. The team did their job of pulling, and the binder moved over the ground, powered by a big single-drive wheel. The binder rattled, shook, shimmied and coughed its way slowly around the field, each binder part doing its assigned task. All of the parts worked together but looked totally unrelated. The wooden *blades* of the reel turned slowly, gently forcing the stalks of a wide swath of standing wheat into the waiting clattering blades. The cut wheat lies on the wide, moving conveyer canvas, to be carried through the machinery with a complicated series of more conveyer canvases. All the parts of the old binder were designed to waste as little of the grain as possible. Lastly, a complicated and intricate part of the binder automatically collects the grain into a neat bundle, heads on one end, stems on the other, then ties each bundle neatly with twine from a large spool made for the purpose. I never did figure out how the binder knew when the bundle was large enough or how the binder knew when to tie off the bundle and cut the string. The bundle then dropped onto a carrier that would hold 8 to 10 bundles at a time. A foot pedal released the carrier, dropping the collection of bundles into neat piles that farmhands would build into "shocks."

I made my way through the already shocked wheat as I headed toward the stock gap wire gate in the corner of the field. The gap opened into our big cow pasture and the potential threat of Old Charlie, the big Jersey bull that always seemed to be between me and our house, a quarter-mile away. I didn't see Old Charlie anywhere this morning, and thought I was safe, but 50 yards or so, before reaching the gate, I glimpsed a movement out of the corner of my eye. At that instant came the unmistakable snort that sounded if it might have been the devil himself. My heart stopped. I froze in my tracks as I slowly cut my eyes to see Old Charlie eyeball to eyeball. He was partially hidden by three or four wheat shocks that were close together. I swear the old bull was waiting to ambush me. His huge head was down, nose close to the ground. Snorting, his front left hoof pawed the earth, throwing dirt clods and dust all over his dark brown back. That bull had muscles that he had never used, and they rippled as he pawed the earth. I figured he was intending to trample me in the dust.

One of the wheat shocking hands had left the gap down; the bull had naturally found the opening and was now about 20 yards away from me. Almost 2,000 pounds of pure meanness was between me and my destination. I had to get to the house and Dad's wrenches, or I knew that he would bust my hide. I had a choice: maybe get trampled by the old bull or get a whooping from Dad. I chose the bull as the lesser of the two threats.

More than once that old bull had chased my mother and me to the safety of one of the stables in the barn. Dad kept a seasoned 2-inch diameter, seasoned, hickory stick handy when he was working Old Charlie. Now, keeping an eye glued to the bull, I slowly backed toward the gap. Charlie was having none of that. With head down and a bellow of rage, wild-eyed and snorting, Charlie charged, looking as big as a freight train, in a galloping cloud of dust. Heart pounding and adrenaline pumping, I jumped aside just in time, and Old Charlie went roaring by, slobbers flying from his mouth. I quickly hid behind a handy shock of wheat. Now a wheat shock offers scant protection against a Jersey bull, but it was better than nothing. Charlie whirled around looking for his target, making more bawling noises, snorting and pawing up big clods of earth with his front hooves.

I stayed out of sight, huddled behind the wheat shock until Charlie got tired of playing cat-and-mouse with me, and went back to grazing the wheat stubble. Finally, in disdain, he turned his rear end to me as he nibbled the occasional green weed. Darting from wheat shock to wheat shock, I edged toward the makeshift gate. Mission accomplished! Keeping an occasional bush and briar patch between me and Old Charlie, I managed to gain enough distance to feel safe enough to hightail it across the pasture to the house for the jug of water and the wrenches. I stopped by the house to tell Mother about Dad's pie request and about Old Charlie and my narrow escape. "Be careful son, that old bull could really hurt you if he cornered you."

Stopping by the toolshed, I found the ball-peen hammer and gathered the necessary wrenches from the toolbox. I ran from the toolshed to the springhouse to fill the water jug and soak the burlap covering as I had for what seemed a hundred times before. I didn't take the time to look for bullfrogs or try to catch a minnow in the springhouse pool as I usually did. The encounter with the bull had cost me way too much time.

The old water jug was as much a part of farming 60 years ago as any farm implement. It was always close by, providing cool water to quench thirsts throughout the farm's growing and harvesting season that ran from early spring through the late fall.

While I was talking to Mother about pies, picking up wrenches at the toolshed and filling up the water jug at the springhouse, I started to worry about how I was going to get past Charlie when I returned to the field. Fortunately, I didn't have to worry. While I was at the house, Lady Luck was definitely on my side; Charlie had found his way back through the gap, joining the rest of the dairy herd on the other side of the pasture, far enough from the gate not to notice my slightly spooked return.

The drama with Charlie was past, and with Dad's requests taken care of, it was back to serious *farmhand* work for me. During grain harvesting season, my job was to follow along beside the binder, pull out the occasional bundle that got jammed in the carrier, and throw it out of the way of the binders' next "go-round." Plus, I kept an eye out for lost and broken binder parts and made sure the twine didn't run out. Of course, my main job was chief water carrier for Dad and the field hands, plus being responsible for fetching tools. All of this is extremely important work for a 9-year-old farm kid.

The Water Jug & The Wheat Field Ballet

If you are under 50 years of age, you likely have little or no idea of what the term "wheat threshing" means, unless, of course, you remember the mention of threshing and "gleaning" in the early childhood Bible stories you learned in Vacation Bible School. And, quite frankly, you may not be at all interested, or care about "wheat threshing," but then again perhaps I have raised your curiosity. If so, will you do a little time-traveling with me back to the 1940s in southern rural America, to dusty country roads and well-tended small farms.

In those days, if you were a farmer, you most likely grew crops of corn, hay and small grain like wheat, oats, and barley. It's late July, hot and dry, and fields of waist-high grain ripple like an ocean in the hot summer wind. The fields are golden and ready for harvest. Ultimately, as part of the harvesting process, the grain has to be separated from the chaff. This was done with a tractor-powered contraption called a *wheat thresher* or simply a thresher. The thresher is at the core of this story of *wheat field ballet*.

It should be noted that although this story concentrates on wheat threshing, other small grains were also threshed the same way.

Wheat threshing was much more than just the mechanical and laborious process of separating grain from chaff and stalks. It was an annual community social event, an opportunity for neighbor to help neighbor. This was a time for family and friends to gather together and share hard but satisfying work. A time to visit, laugh, joke and yes, to sweat profusely and choke on billowing dust as farmers labored to harvest the grain bounty from the seeds that they had planted in the springtime. Seeds that would sprout, spring up from the soil and grow to maturity, spring up, that is, if good fortune smiled on the farmer, and the rains fell and the sun shone at just the right time.

Farmers filled burlap bags with threshed wheat and sold a portion of it to the miller at their local flour mill for cash to buy a few of life's necessities and farm supplies. The rest of their wheat was ground into flour. Their oats and barley could be ground at the local feed mill to feed to their livestock. Each year, farmers held back an ample quantity of their best grain from the harvest for seed, and carefully stored it away for the next year's crop. This was long before giant corporations developed genetically enhanced grain hybrids that they trademark to prohibit more than one growing season.

A few weeks before threshing time, farmers with horse-drawn binders would pull into the wheat field and proceed to cut the grain stalks a few inches above the ground, tie it into bundles (sheaves), then dump the bundles in piles of 8 to 10. Neighbor farmers followed the binder, carefully standing several bundles on end with all the grain heads coming together at the top and resting against each other to form a substantial "pyramid" that wouldn't fall over. They would then lay 2 or 3 more bundles across the top of the pyramid, stems fanned out slightly to form a sort of protective covering – all in a process called "shocking." The shocks of wheat were left standing in the fields for several days to cure out, eliminating all traces of moisture before threshing, as even a slight amount could cause the grain to mold in the bag and become worthless.

In our farming community, two middle-aged bachelor brothers named Joe and Leonard Welch ran the thresher contracting business. During the grain-harvesting season, they traveled throughout the community, going from farm to farm, threshing wheat and other small grain. The thresher was pulled by a huge, old McCormick Deering tractor that had been manufactured in the mid 1920s, and the thresher would have been manufactured around the same time. Besides their threshing operation, the "Welch Boys," as they were called, ran the local blacksmith shop plus a steam engine-powered sawmill.

The thresher was a big, awkward looking mechanical marvel of its time. It looked like a steel, tin, canvas and wood version of some prehistoric creature that roared and belched dust and straw when it was in operation. The exterior of the beast was covered with heavy galvanized sheet metal, reinforced with iron. Dozens of pulleys of varying sizes protruded from both sides of the machine.

All of the pulleys were interconnected with drive belts, some with a single twist, and some straight, but all necessary, each doing a specific function in the overall process of separating grain from straw and chaff. I never could figure out how Joe and Leonard remembered exactly where and how every belt went, and I never saw them use any sort of installation diagram, but the thresher always seemed to run the way it was supposed to.

It was quite a chore just to get the lumbering beasts of tractor and thresher down the narrow country gravel roads and into the fields where the work was to be done. Due to the width of the machinery, gates usually had to be removed or a section of fence taken down. The thresher sometimes arrived the afternoon before actual threshing day, as it took time to "set" the thresher and position the tractor. Shallow pits had to be dug for the thresher's wheels to drop into to keep it from moving. The tractor was positioned 100 feet or so from the front, or "business end," of the thresher with the big drive pulleys of both tractor and thresher in perfect alignment. This positioning could take several attempts, as the single heavy drive belt (with one twist) had to be perfectly aligned between tractor and thresher, or it would "walk" itself off the drive pulleys, creating a disastrous tangle of belts, men, mules and wagons.

On the "business end" of the thresher, the hinged feeder that had been folded down for road travel was now lifted into place and locked. In operation, bundles of grain were pitchforked from the wagons onto the moving canvas feeder, and this was the beginning of the actual threshing process.

On the back end of the thresher, a large, 25-inch diameter, 20-foot long, stacking pipe was hand-cranked into position. The big pipe could be cranked left, right, up or down. An adjustable hood at the straw-stacking "business" end of the pipe, controlled with hand cranks and adjustment wheels was accessed by a crewman standing on the top of the thresher. This gave the stacker operator control of the location, size and shape of the straw stack.

The metal *grain sacker* was located approximately midway down one side and attached near the top of the thresher. This too was a single metal tube, 10 to 12 inches in diameter, becoming an inverted "Y" at the bottom end which stopped 3 feet or so short of the ground. A hand-operated shut-off flip lever at the apex of the "Y" allowed a person to control the flow of grain to either leg of the "Y." A burlap bag was attached by hooks to each leg of the "Y", and when one bag was full, the lever was flipped over, and the grain would flow into the second bag. The full bag could now be removed from the hooks and replaced with an empty bag ready to fill. The tops of the full bags were sewn shut with a special sack needle and strong twine string, then moved to one side, all to be loaded on wagons later in the day for the trip to the farmer's granary.

Everything was ready for threshing day, and the only thing left was to pray that it wouldn't rain overnight.

We got up early on the morning of threshing day, completed all the barn chores, harnessed and hitched the mules to the hay wagon that did double-duty as a "thresher wagon." Dad and I were in the field by the time the morning's early, hot July sun had burned off most of the dew. We parked the wagon and team close to the thresher to wait until the shocks of wheat were completely dry.

Joe and Leonard came bouncing across the wheat field stubble in their faded grey 1936 International, *ton and a half* flatbed truck, arriving in the field just after Dad and me. They oiled or greased every moving part of the thresher, then fueled up the big red tractor from a fuel tank on the back of their truck.

Over the next few minutes, several neighbors with their wagons and pitchforks joined us. They were *swapping work* with us, helping to bring in our wheat crop; then we in turn would move from farm to farm helping each of our neighbors until all the grain in the community was harvested.

The neighbors' kids that were old enough came along to help out and to have the fun of participating in the "threshing adventure." Wheat threshing wasn't all play for us kids because it was our responsibility to make sure a jug of cool, fresh spring water was always available. Fresh water always had to be close by to cut the dust from the throats of the thresher crew. About every five minutes, or so it seemed, we were warned to stay a safe distance from the wagons, teams and machinery and to run to the springhouse and fill up the burlap-wrapped glass jug with fresh water. A bunch of hard-working thresher hands sure could drink a lot of water in the run of a day.

"Let's thresh some wheat, boys," Leonard Welch called out as he turned the hand crank, starting the old tractor that then sat idling until the first load was brought alongside the thresher. Wagon crews moved out and started loading up the wagons with bundles of wheat. Usually there were three men to a wagon, one on each side, alternately tossing up bundles with pitchforks, and one on the wagon, carefully stacking the bundles as high as was possible without the load tipping over or sliding off, as this occasionally happened with a poorly stacked load.

As the wagons were loaded, they were driven to the thresher and lined up behind each other. The lead wagon's team was coaxed to bring the load close alongside the thresher and parallel to the feeder. As the thresher is fed, dust spews from every seam; belts spin; pulleys hum; and straw belches from the big stacker pipe. The entire machine seems to be alive, heaving, snorting and rattling. The vibrating and roaring of the monster has spooked many a good wagon team and caused them to run away, dumping the loaded wagon as they went. A thresher is a lot for a team to endure, and only trained mules and horses needed to apply for the job.

Wagons in position, the wagon driver stood on top of the loaded wagon with pitchfork in hand; it was his job to fork one bundle at a time into the feeder, keeping it full and making the process move smoothly. The feeder's wood slat and canvas conveyer pulled the bundles into the heaving, growling innards of the machine.

As you watch this harvesting of grain called *wheat threshing*, you come to realize that what you're witnessing has a rhythm, a flow, a wonderfully natural choreography. With a fluid movement not unlike that of a ballet, or modern dance; though likely no farmer that I knew would have ever considered this as anything but hard, dust-choking work. Most would think that I was daft in the head for the mere thought of comparison.

You could almost hear the background orchestration as the wagons rolled slowly from shock to shock, farmers walking on each side, their pitchforks moving bundles of wheat from ground to wagon in a steady rhythm. The wagons moved from field to thresher and back again. On each side of the thresher, a farmer stood on top of the wagonload of wheat, feeding bundles of wheat into the machine. The up, down, back-and-forth rhythm of the stacker builds the straw stack. The rhythm of the sacks as they are filled with golden grain, switched out, sewn shut, set aside and replaced with an empty bag all in continual repetition.

While the farmers were tending their threshing chores, their *wheat field ballet*, back in the farm kitchen, wives, mothers, grandmothers and daughters were doing their own *dance*. Each person moved with a rhythm and a fluid motion, staying out of each other's way as they prepared a veritable country feast. They were preparing fresh vegetables from the garden, canned sausage from the cellar, and country ham from the smokehouse, cured from last winter's hog killing. They were cooking fried chicken, roast beef and corn on the cob. We always had cornbread, biscuits and white "loaf" bread that sat on the table in its wrapper. For dessert, we had peach cobbler, chocolate pie and banana pudding, all washed down with gallons of sweet tea cooled with ice chipped from a 50-pound block from the wooden icebox. A country feast cooked on a wood-burning kitchen stove, prepared and placed on a "sawhorse" table of long boards covered with oilcloth of red-and-white or blue-and-white checks. The "table" was placed under big maple shade trees where a summer breeze could usually be found. After lunch (we called it dinner), and with a full belly, the final glass of iced tea, and a chance to rest for a few minutes, doze, smoke a pipe or Lucky Strike cigarette, it was back to the fields and the job at hand.

Call it a ballet, call it a dance, but whatever you want to call it, there was an unmistakable rhythm that incorporated repetitive and fluid movement of man, animal and machine. Then add to that dust, noise, sweat and a little potential danger as all these elements came together. Toss into the mix women in the kitchen cooking, moving in rhythm as they prepared the meal for the thresher crew. Then what better to call it than the wheat field ballet?

THE WATER JUG & HAY CUTTIN' TIME

After all the evening chores were done and we had finished eating our supper of dinner leftovers; Dad and I continued to sit at our regular place at the table. Dad and Mother would talk while she cleared the table and washed the dishes. Dad smoked his pipe, and I worked on my homework. Once the dishes were washed and put away, Mother would join us after retrieving her embroidery hoop and brightly colored thread from her rocker in the keeping room.

The keeping room was a combination living room and Mother and Dad's bedroom. This was a usual living arrangement for country folks when I was growing up. Dad would refill his crooked stem pipe with Prince Albert smoking tobacco from the bright red tin with a photo of Prince Albert gracing each side.

Time for me to sit quietly and listen to them talk as they shared the day's events, and those times long gone by. I sat at the table and continued on my homework by the light of the coal oil lamp as the flickering flame cast shadows on the walls. They would talk of their childhood, family, neighbors and who in the community was sick and needed help, and during the course of the evening the conversation would usually turn to the current season of the year and the farm work coming up.

"The lespedeza hayfield in the bottom land next to Bob Murdock's alfalfa field is ready to cut," Dad said, leaning his straight chair back to balance precariously on two legs, as was his habit. Bob Murdock owned the farm adjoining us. Pulling another long draw from his old pipe and talking around the smoke, he said, "We'll listen to the weather forecast in the morning on John McDonald's Farm Report, but I think that the good weather may hold for a few more days." John McDonald was the host of a popular farm report that was broadcast at 5:00 a.m. on WSM radio, beamed from Nashville, Tennessee. "If I can cut hay tomorrow, let it cure for a day, we can start raking and hauling it to the barn, day after tomorrow. We can start just as soon as the dew dries off the hayfield, and that should be no later than mid-morning." Mother nodded her head in agreement, but her concentration and attention were focused on the flower and bluebird pattern that she had traced on the pillowcases that she was embroidering.

Cutting and "putting up" hay is a simple farm chore. Basically, you just cut it down, let it cure, rake it up, and load it on a wagon. Wagon loaded, you haul it to the barn, and put it in the loft. Those few seemingly simple acts of harvesting set in motion a whole series of actions and activities. Thing was, this particular hay-cutting time was before the use of tractor-drawn rakes and hay balers at our place, so we hauled loose hay using pitchforks and horse-drawn equipment to move it around.

———•———

A few weeks before actual hay-cutting day and taking advantage of a couple of rainy weekends, Dad had checked and replaced any of the broken or worn-out parts on the hay harvesting equipment; mower, rake, wagons, even the horses' harnesses and shoes. He replaced or sharpened broken and worn mower blade sections. The triangular, sharp-edged sections were held in place by two rivets and could be removed from the cutter bar by taking hammer to chisel and cutting the rivets. Replacement sections were held in place by new rivets. The old usable sections that remained on the cutter bar were sharpened with a hand-powered sharpening grinder made for the purpose. I cranked the grinder, and Dad held the long mower cutter bar, with all the sections attached, at just the right angle to sharpen each section individually. Once sharpened, Dad slipped the cutter bar back into its guides, being careful not to lose a finger in the process, and attached it to a wooden drive shaft called a "pitman." One end of the pitman was attached, off-center, to a drive wheel, and the other end, a sort of steel ball and socket, was attached to the end of the cutter bar that was closest to the mower. The pitman provided the *push-pull* motion that made the cutter bar do its job.

———•———

The "dump" hay rake was given the once-over and checked to make sure that all the moving parts actually moved. This horse-drawn piece of ingenuity had a high iron seat positioned at the center between two equally high iron wheels. From this perch, the driver controlled the team and the rake's action and could easily look back at the rake's hay accumulation. The business part of the rake was behind and below the driver's seat. A row of spring-loaded teeth all the same size formed a large open, partial circle about 3 or 4 feet in diameter. Made of spring steel about a half-inch in diameter, each rake tooth culminated in a moderately sharp point and collectively formed a sort of "rake tooth tube" that ran full length between the rake's wheels. The points dragged the ground, collecting hay until the row of teeth were filled; then the driver stepped on a foot pedal that activated the raising and then the lowering of all the teeth in unison. The object was to release the raked hay to form long rows called *windrows*. Once this was done, the rake was turned down the rows, piling hay into shocks, which would be *pitchforked* up to the wagon.

The two-horse John Deere farm wagon's regular green, wooden box bed had been removed from the bright red running gear. (The running gear consisted of four iron-rimmed wooden wheels, the axle, wagon tongue and a coupling pole that essentially held the front wheels and back wheels together.) Single trees, one on each side of the wagon tongue were attached to a double tree that was then attached to the front of the wagon's running gear and spanned the width of the wagon. The team was hitched to the single trees by chains called "trace" chains. A fifth wheel attached to the front axle of the wagon let the front wheels freely turn left and right. The box bed was replaced with a "hay frame" made of wood with "slat wings" that extended a few feet past the full length of the running gear; most of the extra length was at the rear of the wagon. The wings flared out from the floor of the bed and were several feet wider at the top than at the bottom. The hay frame was open at both ends, but the front was punctuated with a removable, vertical hitching pole. The pole was tall enough to wrap the leather wagon lines around and then loop through a deep notch cut in to the top of the pole. The line pole held the lines in easy reach of the man on the wagon, even when the wagon was fully loaded with loose hay.

———•———

Early on the morning of hay cuttin' day, soon as the sun broke red gold above the distant hills and long before the dew was gone, Dad was tending to business. He moved around and over the old horse-drawn mower, greasing and oiling everything that moved. That old mower had moving parts, lots of them. With all equipment having been previously checked and repaired; Dad harnessed the horses, two big bay Percheron mares with white feet, and hitched them to the mower. They were stamping their hooves in place, nodding their heads, snorting and eager to be about the business of cutting hay. As soon as the morning sun dried the dew, with the cutter bar guide lifted and bolted in place for traveling to the hayfield, Dad was in the driver's seat of the mower. With reins in hand, slapping the horses gently across the rear, Dad called, "Kate and Polly, let's get after it now, ladies." He always talked gently to his team, usually just barely above a whisper. He had no time for men who yelled, slapped and otherwise were abusive to their teams. I did see him get so mad at a stubborn mule once that he hit the mule between the eyes with his fist, knocking the mule out colder than a cucumber. The mule was a lot more agreeable when he regained consciousness, but I think Dad always felt really bad about hitting the mule so hard. He thought that he had killed the critter.

Dad, mower and team headed down the lane that led to the hayfield a quarter-mile away, with me trotting along behind, trying to dodge the cow patties and stickers with my bare feet. Once in the field, Dad tied the team's lead rope to a handy bush in the fencerow. He and I started walking around the edge of the field to make sure there were no rocks or stumps that might break the mower or groundhog holes that might cause a horse to break a leg.

Completing our walk around the edge of the field and returning to the mower, Dad untied the team. He dropped the cutter bar guide to cutting position and slid his tall frame into the iron mower seat. Grabbing the lines, he encouraged the horses, and the mowing began. With a fast *klackaty, klackaty, klackaty,* the cutter bar rapidly moved back and forth on the guides. He first mowed around the outside edge of the field, following along where we had just made our inspection walk. Then he turned the mower and team in the opposite direction to mow the field from the outside in. While he was mowing, my job was to keep circling the field to wind up in the middle. I stayed ahead of the mower to make sure there were no stumps, rocks or sinkholes in the entire field that would cause trouble for the team or the mower. Dad had rented the hayfield from a neighbor and was unfamiliar with what obstacles might be hidden by the tall lespedeza hay.

At the age of 9, I was a bit too young to be much of a *hay hand,* but I still tagged along, doing what I could, following behind the hay wagon and making water runs to the well in our yard, filling the burlap-wrapped, glass gallon jug with cool, fresh well water. I'll bet that I made more than a hundred trips to the springhouse or well to fill that jug with fresh water for Dad and the field hands.

By the time I was 11 or 12, I was old enough to make a passable hand, plus Dad usually hired two or more neighbors to help out during hay-cutting season. Sometimes the farmers in the community "swapped work," moving from one neighbor's fields to the next until everyone's hay was in the barn.

———•———

I finished my "field inspection" by mid-afternoon, and Dad continued to cut hay all day, only taking out time to eat dinner and to water the horses at the pond that was close to the barn. During dinner, the horses were left in the shade of a big beech tree in the barnyard, their lead ropes tied to a low-hanging limb with enough slack for them to graze a short distance. There they stood, patient, heads down, dozing, switching flies with their tails, stamping their hooves when a big horsefly bit too hard and drew blood, and occasionally jerking their heads and sneezing gnats from their nostrils.

After a dinner of pinto beans, fried corn, fried okra, country ham, cornbread and fresh-sliced tomatoes, all washed down with big glasses of sweet tea, it was time for a 30-minute rest in the shade of the big water maple that grew in our side yard. Officially, it was to give time for dinner to settle, but actually it was just enough time to rest a bit and to enjoy a roll-your-own smoke before untying the horses and going back to the hayfield.

By sundown, all the hay was cut and lying on the ground, along with a chicken snake that the clattering cutter bar had dispatched. Three fur-lined rabbits' nests had been mowed over, each nest with two tiny babies with white stars in the center of their foreheads and so young their eyes were yet to open. The nests were in a shallow "rabbit hole" in the ground, and fortunately the babies were unharmed, just barely missed by the clattering blade.

I'm sure that when the mother rabbit returned, she was hysterical and immediately moved the babies to a much safer location.

Hay has to have enough time after cutting to "cure" or dry out before storing, but not so much that the leaves all fall off the stems. If you put hay, loose or baled, in the barn while damp or before the sap dries sufficiently, it will sometimes heat to the point of bursting into flames, burning down the barn. Many barns have been lost from wet or uncured hay. In our case, the summer heat cured the hay quickly, and within a day after cutting, the hay was ready for the barn loft.

———•———

The hay had been curing for a full day after being cut, and as soon as the dew was gone the following morning, Dad, team and rake were in the field. Time for the old rake to do its job and Dad expertly handled the team, so that in a few hours the rake had made piles, or *shocks*, of loose hay over the entire field. While Dad was raking, neighbor wagons with their teams and crews started to load hay. One hay hand, an expert at placing each fork full of hay at just the right place, was on the wagon. He was responsible for building the load so it wouldn't fall off. The wagon was driven between shocks so that the two hay hands walking along either side could "pitchfork" the shocks up to the man on the wagon. This was done in an alternate rhythm, so the person stacking the wagon wouldn't be covered up in hay. As they moved from shock to shock loading hay, the load grew higher and higher and built out over the wings of the hay frame. When the last fork full of hay was loaded and in place, the wagon and crew headed to the barn loft to unload.

The hay wagon was pulled alongside of the barn, parallel to and centered below the door to the hayloft. We tossed the hay into the hayloft window, and the hay hands transported forks full of hay to the back of the loft, stacking the hay to the roof as they went. It was not unusual to see lofts completely filled to the very top with loose hay. You haven't lived until you are standing on top of the haymow, up to your waist in loose hay. You're so close to the barn's tin roof that you have to stoop, enduring hay chaff down your collar, trying to dodge red wasps with a really nasty attitude, while the temperature is hovering around 115 degrees.

Each night during hay season we filled Mother's big zinc washtub with cool water from the well for Dad and me to take turns taking a bath, ridding ourselves of the accumulation of dust and the hay chaff that always found its way down the back of our shirts and caused us to itch like crazy, and always in places we couldn't reach to scratch.

Most of the barns in our community had built-in hayfork systems, and that was a big help. Mechanical hayforks were marvelous inventions that ran back and forth on a track that was suspended in the very top of the loft and ran the full length of the barn. The track actually extended 6 to 8 feet past the loft at the front of the barn, which was protected by a covered portico extension of the roof. The fork moved on track rollers, the back-and-forth movement controlled with a long, heavy, 2-inch diameter hay-fork rope that attached to the fork on one end and to the harness of a horse or mule on the ground on the opposite end of the barn from the hay wagon. The horse or mule was controlled by a farm hand, while the man on the hay wagon controlled the action of the fork. The fork was somewhat like a huge needle, sometimes single and sometimes double. I don't remember exactly how the thing worked, if actually I ever knew, but I do know that the fork was controlled with a short length of rope and flip levers. The operator could pull the fork along the track to just where it needed to be, over the hay wagon. The fork was pulled down to the wagon, positioned and then was pushed down into the selected part of the hay load. A spreading hook mechanism could be flipped out a few inches above the point of the fork, designed to keep the hay from falling off.

Fork full, the man on the wagon would yell, "loaded," alerting the pull team that the fork was loaded and ready to move. The fork with its hay load ascended to the track, then was pulled along to its destination in the loft. The destination of each loaded fork was determined and controlled by the men in the loft issuing directives to the farm hand working with the pull-horse. They would yell at the driver to stop, and the hands would release the hay exactly where they wanted. The hay fork was quite a mechanical marvel in its day and saved many man hours, as a full load of hay could be unloaded in less than half the time it took to unload the wagon, one pitchfork full at a time.

As afore mentioned, during "hay season," farmers often swapped work, meaning simply that a crew of neighbors helped each other get the hay in the barn, moving from farm to farm until the work was completed.

As the men swapped work, so did the women, moving from one neighbor's kitchen to the next following the hay hands as they moved from one farm to the next. The unsung heroes of hay season were the women who cooked dinner for the hands, gathering vegetables from the garden, opening jars of canned fruits and vegetables, sweating in an un-air-conditioned kitchen over a wood-burning cook stove and always seeming to have a great country meal, complete with multiple desserts on the table at exactly high noon every day.

The hayloft was a great place for farm kids to play, and I have wonderful memories of rainy days spent in the loft, where my playmates and I jumped from high support beams into the soft pile of hay. As our imaginations soared we were transformed into Superman, Captain Marvel or some other comic book or radio serial hero of the day. I wonder if any kid today would swap their video games for spending an afternoon jumping into loose hay, letting their imagination run wild. I guess not...

END

BILLY, CLYDE AND
A MULE NAMED "LOU"

When the old wind-up Waterbury alarm clock started its early morning clanging wake-up ritual, it was still dark outside. At 4:00 a.m., the inky-black, pre-dawn foretold of a sunup lying just below the eastern horizon, already flirting with the early morning sky. I pried one eye open and could see the morning star through my open bedroom window at exactly the same moment Dad called from the kitchen, "Billy, get up Son, it's almost daylight." I wasted no time jumping out of bed, throwing on a shirt, leaping into my overalls and lacing up my brogan shoes before running down the stairs to meet Dad at the back door. With the coal oil lantern in his hand, we started down the narrow dirt path to the barn. While he fed the mules, and put cow feed for each dairy cow in the concrete trough running the length of the dairy barn, I was stumbling around in the night pasture trying to avoid fresh cow patties and sticker weeds as I rounded up the cows to drive them toward the barn.

By 4:30 a.m., all nine milk cows were fastened in their stalls in the dairy barn, munching contentedly on their morning ration of crushed corn mixed with blackstrap molasses. Dad and I each had homemade wooden milk stools and stainless steel milk buckets, and we milked each cow by hand. Milking was not a lot of fun as you were subject to swats across the face with a cocklebur-laden cow tail, an occasional cow hoof in the milk bucket, or even having the milk bucket kicked over by a flying hoof. As we milked each cow, we poured the milk into the cotton filter-lined steel strainer that sat on top of the milk can. When the can was full, we moved the strainer to an empty can. The milk was filtered cleanly into 10-gallon steel milk cans, each with our special numbers carefully brush-painted on the side in bright red.

Every farm had its own identifying numbers, and those numbers told the milk truck driver and the processing plant which cans belonged to each farm. After we completed the milking, we set out the milk cans on a wooden platform that was easily accessible to the milk truck. The platform was close to the same height as the floor of the milk truck, so the "can puller" had an easier job of pulling the 80-pound cans onboard. It isn't easy to lift the weight of a full milk can shoulder high to load it from the ground to the truck. I speak from experience. I was a "can puller" the summer I was 15. The truck would pick up full cans for the trip to the milk plant and leave behind empties from the day before that had been steam cleaned. Early on, the milk truck ran twice a day in the summer to keep the milk from spoiling. Later, dairy farms were required to have a cooling room with a milk cooler filled with cold water, and the "can puller" had to load the truck with cans straight from the cooler.

After we fed and milked the cows, we drove them down the cow chip-festooned lane that ran from behind the barn to the pasture a couple of hundred yards away. With the cows turned out to pasture, the milk buckets and strainers washed, we scooped out the manure and added it to the big manure pile at the back of the barn. After we finished hosing and scrubbing the barn clean, we headed for the house. It was now approaching 6:30 a.m., and we were about half-starved and ready for Mother's good country breakfast of fried side meat, white milk gravy, eggs, fried potatoes, biscuits and homemade jelly.

"I can smell that good side meat cooking all the way out here," Dad said.

"Yep, me too," I replied. "Makes me even hungrier than I was already, and I was already just about starved."

The clean smell of the fresh crisp morning still hung in the air that early spring day. Rays of the morning sun were shining through the starched, white lace kitchen curtains, which cast a soft yellow glow over the entire kitchen. A light breeze coming through the open window rustled through the curtains.

Finishing breakfast and "full as a tick," I pushed the last round slice of fried potato around with my fork, trying to decide if I could hold that one last bite. The old battery radio was tuned to WSM as always, and Bradley Kincaid was singing, "The Story of Robin Red Breast." Mother loved that song and would sing along as she cooked breakfast or washed the dishes. Dad finished his last bite of one of Mother's spoon biscuits he had slathered with homemade churned butter and molasses, washing it down with a final swallow of milk-laced coffee. Then he gave me a "let's go to the field" look as he grabbed his old sweat-stained, tan work cap from the back of his ladder-back kitchen chair. The screen door slapped shut behind me as we headed back down that familiar path to the barn.

I walked a few feet behind Dad, all the while keeping an eye out for our big Rhode Island Red rooster. He was a mean son-of-a-gun with a very serious hair-trigger attitude flaw, and he was hell-bent on flogging me whenever he had a mood swing and the opportunity. He seized the opportunity real often. Dad threatened more than once to send the rooster to the "Sunday Dinner" pot; ultimately, the day of reckoning came for the old rooster and Dad did just that. One morning, on the path to the barn, as the old rooster was right on my heels and preparing to strike, Dad, from a few yards in front of me and the old rooster, let fly with a handy stick of stove wood, whacking the cantankerous bird, breaking his neck.

"Well, now," Dad said, "looks like you and Mother are going to have rooster, dumplings and dressing for dinner today."

Mother served it up with a bit of poetic justice for me. Dad didn't like chicken.

Even though the morning sun was on the horizon, it was still dark in the barn hall, and Dad paused long enough to light the coal oil lantern and hang it on a nail. He took the bridle off its peg, opened Lou's stall, slipped the bridle over the mule's head and fastened it before leading her into the hall. He threw the plow harness onto the back of the mule and buckled it in place, snapping the short leather lead line into the bridle ring. Then with one arm, he hoisted me up onto the old Jenny mule's broad back. I held on to the harness with both hands as Dad reached for the lead line and clucked to Lou, and our little procession headed for the hillside field that lay a few hundred yards behind our house.

Dad had already spent several days turning the rich dark brown soil of the rocky "new ground" field. This was land he had worked to clear of scrub bushes, saplings and briars over the past winter with the intent to plant the field in corn. The morning sun was casting streamers of red, gold and lavender against the pale blue green of the eastern sky as I slid from the back of the mule to the ground. Dad wrapped the plow lines around his hands, grabbed the plow handles and gently encouraged Lou with a throaty "let's get out now Lou." After a lurching start, the big mule pulled the "bull-tongue" plow along easily and steadily as the slick, shining plow point cut its way deeply through the earth, turning the bright green spring grass and yellow dandelion flowers under. Sprigs of green poked through here and there, contrasting richly with the dark brown of the earth.

Dad would "sight line" our mule and plow to a bush or fence post on the far side of the field to keep his furrows arrow-straight. He was darn near obsessive about straight furrows and rows and a weed-free cornfield. These were sources of great personal pride that he and other farmers in the community shared, and there was a lot of spoken, and unspoken, competition among them. Rows and furrows were things farmers good-naturedly compared and bragged about as they sat on the front porch over at Wade's country store, the community grocery and gathering place, on Sunday mornings.

"Hey Clyde," old man Bradford would sometimes tease, "I saw your cornfield was full of weeds this morning on my drive over here. Heh...heh...heh." It was generally acknowledged by most of them that Dad's fields were the straightest, most orderly and weed-free in the community.

As I followed a few paces behind Dad, walking the plowed furrow, the cool earth felt good to my bare feet. I walked with my head down, my concentration intense. I was looking for Indian arrowheads, "Indian money," unusual rocks or anything that might prove "prehistoric." I had been reading about Indian artifacts and all sorts of prehistoric stuff in the books that I had borrowed from the meager supply at the two-room neighborhood schoolhouse that I attended in the first and second grade. As I was an "expert" in such matters, I was sure that Dad was going to plow up some of the stuff that I had been reading about. Over the past year or two, with some helpful additions from my granddad, Pap Crabtree; I had collected enough arrowheads, spear points and bits and pieces of chipped flint stone to almost fill a cigar box. As I continued to walk in the furrow behind Dad, something caught my attention out of the corner of my eye. Right on top of the plowed ground was a black and yellow rock that to my discerning eye was obviously "prehistoric."

With all my vast experience and "expertise," I had never seen anything like this. Quickly picking up my find, I sat down immediately to study my prize in detail. "Hmmmm," I said to myself, both curious and anxious as I examined it further. This was no rock after all, but instead was some sort of black and yellow prehistoric shell. By this time Dad, mule and plow were quite a distance from me. I examined my treasure more closely, and I noticed a small crack in the shell. As I held it up close to my face and peeked through the tiny opening, I saw two vicious-looking claws attached to what appeared to be a pair of scaly feet and a pair of small, black beady eyes glaring back at me. I yelped with terror and rolled down the hill in one direction as I threw the shell in the other. I got to my feet and ran as fast as I could, adrenalin pumping, to catch up with Dad and Lou.

A few yards away from Dad, I gasped and choked out a description of this "thing" that I had found. He stopped Lou and pushed his cap back on his head, looked me in the eye and said, "Why don't you run on back and pick up your "prehistoric find" and let's have a look at it."

Hesitating for a moment and thinking to myself: "Nope, not me. I'm not going back to pick up that thing, because without a doubt, there is a vicious animal in that shell."

"Son," my dad said, amused but stern, "there ain't a thing in that shell that's gonna hurt you; now do like I tell you and go on back there and pick it up and bring it here."

I was more scared of Dad than I was the critter. So, slowly and with the cold fear of impending doom tap-dancing up and down my spine, I approached the "beast" carefully and gingerly picked it up.

I took off running back to Dad as fast as my 7-year-old legs could carry me, my heart racing as though it was going to jump through my chest. By this time, Dad was sitting on the tongue of the plow, a sack of Country Gentleman tobacco in one hand and a cigarette paper in the other. As he rolled his cigarette with second-nature precision, he nodded his head and said, "Now, set your rock, or shell, or whatever you think it is on the ground down there so we can keep an eye on it for the next few minutes."

Still breathing hard and as nervous as a cat, I did as he asked, and after a few minutes, what looked to be a small trap door started to drop down. A tiny, beaked head and little feet with sharp claws started to emerge. A little more time passed, and with four legs and its head exposed, my "prehistoric" critter started to walk away.

Dad said, "Son, your "prehistoric" critter is a dry-land terrapin or box turtle, as some folks call it, and probably one of the gentlest creatures on earth. Now let that be a lesson you carry with you— never pick up anything unless you know what it is in the first place."

The terrapin slowly went his own way, climbing over the fresh-plowed earth, a bit confused and thrown off course by having been picked up, peered at, tossed across the field and then retrieved for additional archeological observation. Dad returned to his position behind Lou and the plow and centered his focus once again on the fence post on the far side of the field. Much wiser, I spent the rest of the day walking the narrow furrows behind Dad, still looking for those extraordinary discoveries I might stumble upon and the fascinating rewards the plowed soil might release from its grip. By milking time, my pockets were filled to bulging with all of the new additions to my growing rock collection.

END

A RAINY DAY
IN THE HAYLOFT

Years ago, a rainy day on the farm meant a day off from serious farm work like planting, plowing and harvesting. Of course, we always had the regular daily farm chores: milking the 15 dairy cows twice a day, by hand; climbing the ladder to the hayloft to throw down hay for the mules; and feeding the squealing hogs in the hog pen their ration of shelled corn. Every evening we filled their wooden troughs with slop made of Purina Hog Feed mixed with water.

Not a lot of real exciting stuff on the farm to keep a young boy occupied on a rainy day, so one's mind tends to wander, and in my case, it sometimes seemed to just plain disappear. After the chores were all done, you were stuck in the house with nothing to do except read a book, maybe do some pencil drawing or stand in the doorway watching through the screen as the rain came down.

Of course, that wasn't always the case. Take the rainy day that I decided to *parachute* out of the barn loft. It started raining before daylight that late spring morning, and it hadn't let up by the middle of the afternoon. Naturally, by then, I had run out of things to keep my short attention-spanned self occupied; so I headed down the muddy path to the barn, running as fast as my legs would carry me, my bare feet slapping the muddy earth. I ran through the rain, getting myself soaked in the process. Fortunately, the weather was warm, and my clothes were dry in no time.

If you know anything about a barn, you know it lends itself to young imaginations, with stalls, a corncrib, harness and feed rooms. You can chase mice, discover baby kittens, and attempt to ride young bucking calves. Try as you might, calves are almost impossible to ride because their skin is so loose. If there is nothing else to do, there's always corn in the crib that needs to be shucked, though shucking corn falls way over on the chore side of the equation. Chores are no fun at all when you are almost 11 years old. Then there's the hayloft, conveniently filled with loose hay or stacked to the roof with bales. Ours was filled with loose lespedeza hay, and it was a great place to play Superman, Captain Marvel or some other super hero.

Just about every barn, ours included, had a hayfork, with its necessary track, located just under the roof in the uppermost part of the hayloft. The hayfork was equipped with a 2-inch diameter hemp rope that was used to pull the fork filled with hay from one end of the loft to the other. The forkful of hay was pulled along the track until it reached its proper destination; then a small release rope was pulled, and the hay dropped in the spot where you wanted it. With that big, handy rope in mind you could climb up to one of the supporting cross-timbers high in the loft and close to the rope. You would reach for the rope, grip it tightly with both hands, and swing out, landing in the big pile of loose hay, just like a flying super hero or Tarzan swinging on a jungle vine. Of course, you had to be careful not to overshoot the hay as the loft floor was rough lumber, and it made for a bone-jarringly hard landing. Plus for some reason old barn loft floors always seemed to have several loose boards throughout, and if you landed on them just right, they could flip up and hit you in the face or you would fall clean through to a stable below. Besides the opportunity for getting considerably bruised up, there usually was a good amount of fresh manure and straw in the stables. Landing in manure and straw was bad enough even though it helped to cushion the fall, but you also ran the risk of getting trampled on by a big work mule that could really get spooked if you dropped in on him unexpectedly.

While playing Superman and flying through the air were a lot of fun for maybe a half-hour or so, I soon got bored swinging on the rope and landing in the hay. Plus, the hay got all down in my shirt, and I was starting to itch. I peeled off my shirt and shook most of the hay out before putting it back on.

Pigeons were always roosting in our loft, and they would find a spot high up on one of the wooden wall plates to build their nest, lay their two eggs and raise their hatchlings. Curiosity getting the best of me, I climbed the makeshift wooden ladder attached to the loft wall up to the wall plate. Then, carefully I inched my way along until I could see the inside of the nest. I had been keeping a regular check on the progress of the eggs, and once again I was disappointed that they were still eggs and not little fuzzy pigeons, like I had hoped. I climbed back down the ladder and sat on the dusty loft floor for a spell, listening to the roar of the rain pelting the barn's tin roof. I gave serious thought to what I was going to do next to keep myself entertained. I was seldom bored for more than five minutes as my imagination could always find something to do, and occasionally it got me into trouble.

I know, I thought to myself, I'll play like I'm an airplane pilot. My imagination took over, at least partially fueled by a black-and-white war movie that I had seen at a Saturday movie matinee a few weeks before. The floor of the loft was transformed into my pilot's seat with an imaginary co-pilot sitting next to me. Our eyes are scanning the skies and the instrument panel, while our hands are steady on the controls of the B-17 bomber. We're flying over enemy territory with a load of bombs. Our mission is to locate and destroy a train loaded with ammunition headed to enemy lines.

Just then, four enemy fighter planes came at us from out of the sun, machine guns blazing, their bullets strafing my airplane. The machine guns on my trusty bomber were all firing away *ackack-ackack*, as my gunner crew springs into action. One enemy plane is hit, then another, and another, all three are going down in flames. The remaining enemy fighter turns tail and runs, but not before a lucky shot takes out one of our engines. The engine is on fire and belching black smoke. The plane is going down, and I yell to my crew, "release the bombs and "bail out!" I will be the last one to strap on my parachute and jump out of my airplane.

I'm standing in the loft window ready to jump to safety, assuming of course, that my *parachute* will open, floating me safely to earth. But wait, I thought, I can't jump, I don't have a parachute. "Time out," I said to myself, as I climbed down the ladder from the loft into the barn hall, then hightailed it to the house to sneak Mother's old black umbrella out of the closet. With the umbrella in hand, it was back to the barn, up the ladder to the loft and my "crashing airplane." I'm back in the loft window, and once again I'm standing in the imaginary doorway of the bomber. I checked once again to make sure all the crew was clear of my doomed aircraft. I must act quickly as I have to jump before the plane crashes and takes me with it to my doom. Will my umbrella "*parachute*" let me float to the earth, or will it send me crashing to earth to become a broken mess of stupidity? Would the umbrella hold me up if I actually held it over my head and jumped? My curiosity won out over what little common sense I might have had. I opened the umbrella over my head, held the curved handle tightly with both hands, took a couple of gulps of air and jumped before I had the chance to "chicken out." As soon as I leaped, that danged umbrella immediately turned wrong-side out and I plummeted to earth, feet-first into the muddy barn lot. Fortunately, it was late spring, and the combination of several rains plus the livestock stomping around in the mud and manure had created a muddy, stinking loblolly. Somewhere I had read that when landing with a parachute you should always "drop and roll." I did my drop and roll in water, mud and manure 2 feet deep.

I wasn't physically hurt except for a few bruises here and there, but my pride and Mother's umbrella were busted up something fierce. I figured that as soon as Mother saw my miserable condition and her umbrella, she was going to bust my hide. And the pouring rain wasn't helping my attitude as I hobbled down the path to the house. I opened the screen door and started to step into the kitchen.

Mother stopped me before my mud-covered shoes could hit the floor with, "WOAH, hold it right there young man, don't you dare step into my kitchen with that mud and manure mess all over you. What in heaven's name have you done? How did you manage to completely destroy my old umbrella? You got yourself some serious explaining to do, Son!"

She stopped talking long enough to take a long breath, while, with trembling lips, I tearfully started to explain the whole sad tale. As I talked, I noticed that she started turning her head away from me. She seemed to be looking at something out the kitchen window. She was kind of shaking and her face looked awfully red, like she was really, really mad. Or maybe, I thought, hopefully, she looks like she's going to bust out laughing any minute. Surely not, I thought as I failed to see anything at all funny about my terrible parachuting misadventure. Maybe she's so angry that she's shaking, I thought.

Gaining her composure as she finally seemed to catch her breath, she said "let's get you out of them wet, nasty, stinking clothes, and you've got to have a washtub bath before you set foot in this house, young man! I may have to burn your clothes 'cause no amount of lye soap and kettle boiling is going to clean them nasty things up."

She didn't send me in search of a perfect switch from the peach tree in the backyard, like I was expecting. I suppose she thought I had been through enough pain and humiliation for one day, and maybe I had learned a valuable lesson out of all this foolishness that I had gotten myself into. She even said, "We better not tell your daddy as he would whoop your butt good. We'll just keep this between us. From now on, I suppose you won't be jumping out of any barn loft windows with an umbrella. The next time you might not be so lucky. The mud might not be as forgiving as it was today. And I know that I won't be, you can depend on that." I'm pretty sure I saw a twinkle in her eye and just a slight hint of a smile.

I wonder, am I the only farm kid that ever made the mistake of jumping out of a barn loft with an umbrella parachute?

END

WALT BRADFORD'S BLACKSMITH SHOP

Walt walked out the front door of his small house with its rusting tin roof, at 6:00 a.m. every morning except Sunday, to walk the half-mile or so down the road to his blacksmith shop. Sunday was his only day to rest and spend time with his girls. Walt and the girls dressed in their best and walked to the nearby United Methodist Church for Sunday School and the 10:30 a.m. preaching service every Sunday morning. Walt didn't own a car, and he figured that as long as he had two good legs, he didn't need one. The blacksmith shop was in the crossroads country village of Delina with its four grocery stores and one service station. Walt's shop was just 150 feet across the dust from Heuie Bigham's big general store with its concrete porch and the usual male assembly. Local sages, political commentators, and liars, mostly made up of retired farmers, could be found holding fort on most any day, especially a rainy one.

The Bradford house was a drab, unpainted gray clapboard with a rickety front porch across the front. The dilapidated screen door had holes in the screen that in summer let in more flies than it kept out. At least a solid, homemade wooden door was behind the screened one, and it would keep out most undesirables that might happen by. The house itself was real close to the county road, and it sat in an unkempt yard filled with tall grass and weeds. From the front steps of the house, a narrow dirt path led to the dilapidated mailbox at the edge of the road. Another well-worn path led to the outhouse that was 30 yards behind the main house. Walt did the best he could at keeping everything going, but sometimes things just didn't get done. Maintaining the yard and the outside of the house wasn't a top priority. He and the girls did keep the yard totally free of any accumulation of trash that came mainly from people tossing stuff from their vehicles as they drove past. But inside, the tiny rooms were kept spotless and replete with a bright red-checked oilcloth on the kitchen table and starched yellow curtains on the windows. Bright flowery spreads were on the beds, and the well-worn linoleum floors were always scrubbed and waxed.

White smoke puffed from the tin flue each morning as Walt prepared breakfast for himself and the girls. The girls were up at the same time as Walt for they had chores to do before they caught the county school bus. The girls were responsible for keeping the house tidy, washing the dishes and most of all, getting good grades in school. Walt believed that the most important consideration of all was that they kept up their grades.

The tin flue from the wood-burning cookstove stuck through a hole halfway up the outside kitchen wall of the house. It ran zigzag up the wall, sticking up a few feet above the comb of the roof, and was held in place with a few strategically placed tie-down wires. The flue gave up its smoke to blend with the early morning fog that hung low over the little valley. The fog dripped from the leaves and turned everything in sight into ghostly silhouettes that faded completely to a damp grey nothingness a short distance away. Early autumn was in the air, and Walt turned up the frayed, tan corduroy collar of his old denim coat against the cool dampness of the morning. He loved the chill that was in the air. This was Walt's favorite time of the year.

Walt shared the little house with his two teenage daughters, Katherine and Marie. Walt's wife, Eudora, the girls' mother, had passed away five years ago, leaving him with the girls to raise. Walt and Eudora also had two sons, John and Tom, who was aptly nicknamed "Tom Cat." Both boys were considerably older than the girls and had long ago moved out of Walt's house to make a life of their own. With Eudora gone and the boys seldom around, the girls were his whole life. Walt struggled to give them the material things that he could ill afford but knew they wanted and needed. He was always concerned that their classmates would make fun of the "dirty blacksmith's kids," so he was often up past midnight washing or ironing clothes. Their dresses might not have been in the pages of the latest fashion magazines, but Walt made sure the girls had clean and pressed clothes for school every day.

Where the girls were starched and ironed, Walt was just the opposite. His skin, hair, gray cotton shirt and overalls always seemed to be covered with a "slick" mixture of grease, sweat and soot. The lines and creases in his face were black "cracks," and even the brown leather cap that sat at a jaunty angle on his great head was slick, dirty and sweat-stained.

Walt's blacksmith shop was a large barn-like structure with a tin roof and unpainted vertical siding of rough-sawn lumber, worn gray with time and the weather. Down one side, midway of the structure, were two large double-wide wooden doors that slid on tracks. Because of the heat from the forge, Walt usually worked with the big doors wide open, winter and summer, to catch any cooling breeze that might find its way through the opening. Out behind the shop was a huge pile of coal that was used to heat the forge, along with a mountain of scrap iron and steel that Walt selected from as the need arose. There were steel rims from wagon wheels, rusting horse-drawn mowers, hay rakes, corn shellers and unidentifiable chunks of iron of no apparent use to anyone, but that became usefully repurposed under Walt's hammer.

Walt's blacksmith shop was as much of a necessity to rural life in the 1930s, '40s, and early '50s as the grocery stores and service stations that made up the rural villages. It was a time when many farmers still farmed with teams and relied on farm equipment made mostly of iron.

Walt made new shoes or reshaped existing ones for horses and mules, then acted as a farrier and trimmed the animal's hooves before nailing the shoes in place. In the remnants of a horse-drawn farming society, he was a mainstay that neighbors depended on. He heat-welded and fitted iron rims of wagon wheels and hub rings. He also made and fitted all metal parts of wagons, carriages and buggies. Walt repaired turning plows, corn planters and cultivators. Most anything made of steel that a farmer could manage to bust; Walt could fix with his forge, anvil, hammer and tongs. Walt was an artisan in iron and steel, heating metal until it was white-hot, then with hammer and anvil, he shaped latches, hinges and butcher knives. And if you had need for an ornamental iron gate or a fancy railing, well, Walt could supply that too. In addition to working in steel and iron, Walt was a fair hand with wood. He could build a wagon bed, rebuild a wagon wheel, repair a wooden axle, make a plow handle or carve an axe handle.

This particular morning, Walt's hand turned the blower handle, forcing air up through the burning coals in the forge; the extra oxygen heated the coals to a bright red, then to a white-hot. He had to make new shoes for Frank Haislip's team of white-nosed, mare mules. Charlie Tipper's two-row corn planter was in the shop for a broken wheel repair. Willie Hobbs' old gray, ton and a half Ford truck needed its right fender beat out, reshaped and re-attached. The fender had gotten ripped off when Willie lost his brakes and hit the gatepost as he was trying to turn into his own driveway. Walt supposed that he would have to try to straighten out the fender and use bolts to re-attach it to the old truck.

With long-handled tongs made of steel, Walt positioned the mule shoes in the forge precisely so as to take advantage of the hottest coals. He kept a sharp eye to the heating horseshoe, and at the right moment he reached for it with the tongs, bringing it from forge to anvil. Holding the shoe with the tongs, he started to size, turn and shape the shoe to one of the mule's hooves with his hammer and a practiced eye. The big hammer showered bright red sparks with each blow. Heating, hammering, shaping, heating, hammering, shaping over and over again, until each shoe fit the mule's hooves exactly. Once shaped to his satisfaction, Walt plunged each of the red-hot shoes into a metal drum (slack tub) filled with water, to cool the steel, stopping the heat process. Then, adding a heavy leather apron to his wardrobe and with his specially made horseshoeing toolbox, Walt proceeded to lift each hoof, grasp it firmly between his knees, trim and file it level and smooth before nailing the shoe in place, always checking to be sure that each shoe was a perfect fit.

Historically speaking, Walt's artistic profession has been around for quite a while. Blacksmithing dates from the earliest Iron Age, which started about 1500 B.C. or earlier in Central Asia. Many of the tools and techniques date from the earlier times of the Bronze Age, going back over 5,000 years. Dating back to Colonial times, the blacksmith was an important part of the community. In 1607 the first colony at Jamestown brought over their own blacksmith.

Walt was a simple man with almost no formal education, and he likely didn't know or care about the long heritage of the blacksmith. He was just trying his best to earn a living and take care of his girls; working at something that he loved and doing what came naturally to him.

As with any professional blacksmith, Walt's "forge" was both a workplace and a hearth. The blacksmith's workplace is sometimes referred to as a "smithy." The basic smithy contains a forge, also known as a "hearth," for heating metals. The forge heats the metal workpiece to a malleable temperature, (a temperature where the metal becomes easier to shape) or to the point where work hardening no longer occurs. The workpiece is transported to and from the forge using tongs. The tongs are also used to hold the workpiece on the smithy's anvil while the he works it with a hammer. Finally the workpiece is transported to the slack tub (a large tub or container of water), which rapidly cools the workpiece. The slack tub also provides water to control the fire in the forge.

Though seemingly simple in nature, the tools and the art of the blacksmith were somewhat more sophisticated than one might expect. Though it was doubtful that Walt would have ever thought of the word "sophistication" being applied to his daily labor.

The following is a description of some of Walt's tools in a bit more detail:

Forge

The open forge was the center of Walt's blacksmith shop, literally. A flue over the forge carried most of the coal smoke to the outside, but plenty of smoke remained to burn your eyes, and sparks to scorch spots on clothes and skin. Walt's forge was standard and used bituminous coal as the fuel to heat metal. His forge was essentially a hearth or fireplace designed to allow a fire to be controlled. The heat of the forge could also bring about other metallurgical effects (e.g., hardening, annealing, and drawing temper). The fire in a forge is controlled in three ways; amount of air, volume of fuel, and shape of the fuel/fire to accommodate different shapes of work.

Anvil

Walt's anvil, which weighed over 300 pounds, was attached by spikes to the flat part of a sawed section of a large hickory log. The log base brought the anvil to the height Walt needed for maximum efficiency. The anvil served as his workbench, on which he placed the metal to beat and shape. Anvils are made of cast or wrought iron with a tool steel face welded on, or the entire anvil could be made of a single piece of cast or forged tool steel. The flat top has two holes; the wider hole is the hardy hole, where the square shank of the hardy tool fits. The smaller hole is the punch hole and is used as clearance when punching holes in hot metal. At one end of the anvil was the "horn," on which Walt shaped metal into a curve.

Tongs

Tongs were used by the blacksmith for holding hot metals securely. The mouths were custom made by the smith in various shapes to suit the gripping of various shapes of metal.

Chisel

Chisels were made of high-carbon steel. They were hardened and tempered at the cutting edge while the head was left soft, so it would not crack and split off when hammered. Chisels were of two types; the cold chisel was used for cutting cold metals, while the hot chisel was for hot metals. Usually, hot chisels were thinner and therefore could not be substituted with cold chisels.

Fuller

Fullers were forming tools of different shapes used in making grooves or hollows. They were often used in pairs; the bottom fuller had a square shank that fit into the hardy hole in the anvil, while the top fuller had a handle. The work was placed on the bottom fuller, and the top was placed on the work and struck with a hammer. He also used the top fuller for finishing round corners and for stretching or spreading metal.

Hardy

The hardy is a cutting tool similar to the chisel. The blacksmith used it as a chisel or hammer for cutting both hot and cold metals. It has a square shank that fits into the hardy hole in the anvil, with the cutting edge facing upward. The metal to be cut is placed on the cutting edge and struck with a hammer. The smith also used it with set tools, which he placed over the workpiece and struck.

Slack Tub

A slack tub is usually a large container full of water, brine or oil used by a blacksmith to quench hot metal. The term is believed to derive from the word "slake," as in "slaking the heat."

These were the tools of Walt's profession, wonderfully simple, yet in the hands of an artist such as Walt, they could help create useful things of steel and iron.

Walt was a giant of a man, standing more than 6 foot 6 inches tall in his high-top boots. His eyebrows and the hair on his arms were constantly singed from the heat and the showering sparks of his occupation, and his big hands were rough, scarred and callused. Years spent with hammer and anvil had built rippling muscles in his arms and shoulders. Walt could have broken a lesser man in two with his bare hands, but fortunately for those around him, he was a friendly, happy man with a thunderous laugh and a booming voice that came from somewhere deep inside. Walt always seemed to have a big "chaw" of Brown Mule chewing tobacco in his cheek, and he could spit a stream of amber tobacco juice with the spot-on precision to hit a crack in the shop's wall 10 feet away. When Walt was in his shop shaping white-hot iron, you could hear the rhythmic ringing sound of hammer to steel from a mile or more away.

Walt's always-full workday ended promptly at 5 p.m., whereupon he would close the sliding doors to his shop, snap the big lock into the heavy, rusty hatch and walk the few yards to Heuie's store. As the sun went down, he would sit on the edge of the high concrete porch, drink his one daily Coca-Cola and spin a fishing yarn and a laugh or two with the regular porch philosophers. Like the ringing iron, his laughter could be heard a mile away. As the sun set, Walt walked the dirt road toward the little house and to the most important thing in his life, his girls. It had been another good day of shaping hot iron.

That was Walt's life—his two girls and shaping white-hot iron.

END

UNCLE TOP & AUNT MAGGIE

Top and Maggie were my father's uncle and aunt, on his father's side, and, to say the least, they were a unique couple.

THIS IS THEIR STORY...

Uncle Top and Aunt Maggie gave true meaning to the term *dirt poor*, but they were proud and happy as a couple of pigs in a mud hole. As a young man, Uncle Top had been as strong as an ox. Around our supper table, Dad would share stories of Uncle Top with my mother and me. And no doubt my father embellished the stories a little bit here and a lot there. But there was one story, in particular, that I remember Dad telling, of how Uncle Top undertook loading a large walnut log onto a wheelbarrow, with the intention of rolling it to a sawmill several miles away. The wheelbarrow immediately collapsed under the log's weight, so Uncle Top hoisted the log to his shoulder and walked the rest of the way to the mill.

By the early 1950s, Top was in his late 70s. *His birth name was Talmage,* and he was still stronger than most men less than half his age. I know because in the early spring I saw him hoist a horse-drawn turning plow to his shoulder. He carried it several hundred yards up a steep hill to a field behind his house. He was planning to put the field in corn.

Although I thought it was a bit strange, I never let on that I noticed Uncle Top's eyes didn't look quite in the same direction.

He seemed to be looking sideways when he was actually looking you straight in the eye. He didn't hear very well, either, so he talked louder than most folks. To be honest, he yelled. Uncle Top's language was quite colorful. He cussed a lot, nearly every breath. 'Course he cleaned it up quite a bit when Mother and me were around, confining it to a liberal sprinkling of "damns" and several "awwww hells."

What few remaining teeth that he had were only on one side of his mouth, and I never remember seeing him without a big *chaw* of chewing tobacco in his cheek. Tobacco juice stained his few remaining teeth, his ever-present week's growth of white beard and the corners of his mouth. He would take the chaw, a large chunk of tobacco cut from a square plug of Brown Mule chewing tobacco, out of his mouth while he ate and lay it beside his plate. Soon as he finished eating his food, the chaw went right back in his cheek.

The sight of that big chunk of already-been-chewed tobacco always left me with a queasy feeling. But I never said anything, and I tried to keep my eyes off the disgusting thing while I ate. Every once in a while during the course of the meal my mother would comment, "Son, you look a little pale; you aren't sick are you?" Of course I couldn't possibly say that the sight of that cud of tobacco was making me sick. Real men didn't let on about such things.

Uncle Top always wore overalls and a gray work shirt. My guess is that he didn't have one pair of Sunday pants or a dress shirt to his name, much less a tie. His work shoes always seemed to be worn way past any real use and were held together with pieces of baling wire or hog rings. If he had any socks he never wore them. Today he was barefoot, and so was Aunt Maggie. She had the biggest pair of calloused feet that I have ever seen on a woman, but Uncle Top had her beat by a country mile. Aunt Maggie was a tall, big-boned woman with long gray hair. She wore her hair pulled back from her face, plaited and then wrapped into a bun at the nape of her neck. There were always a few wisps that escaped the plaits. She had a few more teeth than Uncle Top, but there was less than one set, total, between them. Aunt Maggie dipped Garret Sweet snuff, and she spit the amber liquid through a gap in her front teeth. She could hit a crack in the back of their old stone fireplace from 15 feet away. Her face was brown and full of wrinkles from working long hours in the sun. She always seemed to have a smile, and you got the feeling that the smile was permanently etched. I never saw Aunt Maggie when she wasn't wearing a homemade apron over a homemade dress.

My family visited with Uncle Top and Aunt Maggie twice, maybe three times a year, always on Sunday. And on this particular Sunday, Dad decided it was time to visit his aunt and uncle once again. It was the middle of summer, and it had been hot and bone-dry for weeks. Pastures were parched; cattle were slab-sided and scruffy. They looked like starvation walking. We spent most of our time hauling water in barrels from the creek to provide what water we could to the thirsty livestock. Finally, we had gotten a good, gentle soaking rain all day and night the Saturday before our Sunday visit.

We loaded ourselves in Dad's 1947 Dodge pickup truck. The five-year-old truck was black with dark blue fenders, and the gear-shift was in the floorboard. Dad drove, Mother sat up front with him, and I rode in the truck bed. "Sit down back there and hold on, so you won't fall out," Dad said as he hit the starter pedal in the floorboard with his left foot, shifted into first gear and pulled slowly out of our driveway and onto the main road. As we traveled, I had a panoramic view of the countryside with its barns, fields and cows that raised their heads from grazing to watch as we passed by. We traveled the muddy gravel roads, around curves, over hills and through valleys, 20 miles to the community of McBurg where Uncle Top and Aunt Maggie lived.

Uncle Top and Aunt Maggie had two kids. Their daughter Wilma Dean was 19, blonde, slightly plump, pretty and bright.

Their son Roy was a big quiet man, somewhat mentally challenged, with a big heart and hands calloused and scarred from hard farm work. Roy was in his 30s and still lived at home, helping his dad out on the farm. Wilma Dean worked nights at General Shoe Factory and took a business correspondence course at home. She was determined to escape the poverty and improve her lot in life. Roy was contented with his life just the way it was.

Dad eased the truck into a grassy area off to the side of the gravel main road just a few yards past the wagon-rutted turn-off to the lane that led to Uncle Top and Aunt Maggie's house. Dad was wearing his Sunday Panama hat, a white short-sleeved shirt, blue dress pants and spit-shined, brown dress shoes. He had worn those same shoes to church every Sunday for 20 years, and they still looked almost good as new. Mother was wearing one of the two Sunday dresses that she owned. This time, it was the pink dress with white collar and cuffs and her open-toed sandals. She had the amber plastic handle of her crocheted handbag in the crook of her left arm and was balancing one of her chocolate pies in her right hand. I was wearing my blue Sunday shirt, seersucker pants and my Sunday Buster Brown shoes.

By the time their house came into view, Mother's and my shoes were covered in mud, and try as we might to stay clean, our clothes were splattered from walking the muddy, deep-cut wagon tracks. As was usually the case in situations such as this, where any chance encounter of mud was involved, Dad remained spotless. I swear he could have fallen head-first into a hog wallow and come out clean and starched.

There was really no explaining, but Uncle Top seemed to always rent run-down ramshackle houses way back in some hollow away from the main road. And this homestead was no exception. If the old house had ever seen the business end of a paintbrush, there was no evidence. The tin roof was rusty, and a piece of clapboard had come loose and was hanging from a single nail, high on the side of the house. One of the windowpanes had been replaced with a piece of pasteboard. Another window was repaired with a wad of rags.

As we got closer to the house, we could see Uncle Top on the front porch. He was sitting on what once had been a front seat "borrowed" from an unidentifiable automobile. "Hot damn, Maggie, look a-yonder who's coming down our lane…it's Clyde, Naomer and Little Billy. Put the goat back on the stove and heat it up; they're likely hungry." There was another dilapidated bench car seat sitting on the porch. What had once been white cotton stuffing was pushing through several holes and rips in the uphol-stery. Butch, Uncle Top's big redbone coonhound, claimed owner-ship of this seat, although he would give it up without too much of a fuss. To complete the porch décor, an old refrigerator had found a permanent home at one end. I could never figure out why the refrigerator was on the porch, as the old house wasn't wired for electricity. I don't think Uncle Top ever rented a house wired for electricity. Aunt Maggie cooked on a wood-burning kitchen stove, and their house was warmed in winter with a big fireplace.

The worn front steps to the house were cut from large lime-stone rocks. Flat rocks served as steppingstones that led to the steps. There was one shade tree in the front yard, a large maple. Most of the maple's limbs were dead from some long-past light-ning strike that had split and blackened a generous portion of the trunk.

A few mixed-breed chickens, a red rooster and two white ducks quarreled and scratched in the dirt, hoping to find a sprig of something to eat. Their endeavor seemed futile, as the yard was completely bare – not a single sprig of grass anywhere. Aunt Maggie kept the yard swept and pulled up any grass that dared to show its blades, plus the ducks and chickens pulled up what she missed.

As we got close to the house, Uncle Top said loudly, "Ya'll come on in here, Clyde, Naomer, ya'll have a seat; Butch, get off that seat; git on outta here now and go find you a shady spot. I'll swear all that dog is fitten' for is eatin' and sleepin.' The only thing that fool dog ever chases is a biscuit. Every time Maggie opens the kitchen door, that dang dog is standing there all sad-eyed, begging for a biscuit and gravy. Hot, ain't it? Billy, you can find a soft spot there on them steps. How ya'll been?"

"I better get this pie in the kitchen, Uncle Top; is Aunt Maggie back there?" asked Mother. "She's in the kitchen heating up some fine goat, just go on in, Naomer," Uncle Top responded. "It was a fat young billy, and it's real tender and juicy. Finest goat that I ever tasted; the meat falls right off the bone," Uncle Top said. "It aughter be about ready."

Daddy said, "We appreciate it, but we ate a big dinner right before we left the house, and I don't think any of us could eat another bite, Uncle Top." We hadn't had a bite to eat since our breakfast at 5:00 a.m., and it was 3:00 p.m. Daddy gave me the evil eye that warned me not to let on that we hadn't eaten anything. Thank goodness he said something as none of us had a real hankering for that boiled goat.

"Billy, come on in here and let me see how much you've grown, honey," Aunt Maggie called from the kitchen. I reached for the screen door that opened to their keeping room. Ancient wallpaper, with a faded pattern of big yellow roses and vertical stripes, covered the walls. On one wall there was a framed color photo of Franklin D. Roosevelt and an old couple dressed in black glared down from an oval frame. Above the fireplace mantel was a calendar with an illustration of Dalmatian puppies playing with a fireman's hat. The calendar was 3 years old. Two kerosene lamps anchored each end of the mantel. On another wall was a small hand-tinted photograph of Wilma Dean and Roy when they were small children. There was one rocking chair and two straight-back chairs, randomly placed in front of a stone fireplace. In one corner of the room was an old iron bed that swayed low in the middle. The bed was covered with a brightly colored homemade wedding ring pattern quilt that brightened the otherwise pitifully dull room. A linoleum rug that most anyone would have considered worn out covered part of the floor. The remaining exposed part of the wood had cracks that you could see daylight through, and I wondered how they kept warm in the wintertime with wind blowing through those cracks.

The doors at the front and back of the house were wide open, and the chickens, ducks and flies wandered in and out at their leisure. In the dining room, a clucking, black-and-white Dominicker hen strode around on the white tablecloth that covered bowls of food left on the dining room table from the noon meal, left there to be eaten at suppertime. As Uncle Top and Aunt Maggie had no refrigerator, I have no idea why the food didn't spoil in those hot days of summer, but it didn't seem to be a problem. "Come on in the kitchen, hon, and see your Old Aunt Maggie...my goodness, child, look how you've grown." She gave me a bear hug, squishing my face into her ample bosom. She smelled of face powder, sweat and snuff, a combination that interestingly enough was not totally unpleasant.

Where's Roy and Wilma Dean, Aunt Maggie?" Mother asked.

"Well, Wilma Dean is working a double shift over at General Shoe in Pulaski this weekend, and Roy is across the hill at a neighbor's farm, helping castrate a bunch of young beef calves," Aunt Maggie replied. Aunt Maggie was never one to dance around a subject. My mother's face flushed a slight shade of red.

Mother's chocolate pie was sitting on the kitchen table, and she kept waving her hand over it, trying to keep the flies away, having little success. "Ain't your momma sweet to bring us one of her wonderful chocolate pies? Here, let's put this pot of goat on the table; holler for Clyde, Naomer, and you all come on and eat," said Aunt Maggie. Not knowing it, but reading Daddy's mind, Mother said, "It looks and smells awfully good, but I'll just take a bite or two, if you don't mind. We just ate a big dinner before we left home, and I doubt if any of us are much hungry right now."

Aunt Maggie spooned the goat out on a plate for Mother, adding a big chunk of cornbread. As she nibbled on the goat, Mother asked, "Billy, you want anything to eat?" "I'd love a piece of that chocolate pie," I said, eyeing that wonderful pie. Mother said, "Aunt Maggie, thank you for warming up the goat; it's wonderful, but if it's all right with you, why don't we go ahead and cut the pie, unless of course, you and Uncle Top are still full from your dinner." Aunt Maggie got a butcher knife from a kitchen drawer. While mother cut the pie into equal portions, Aunt Maggie brought enough plates to the table for everyone – most were chipped, and none matched. Mother put a generous slice of pie on each plate. The pie looked wonderful, and the boiled goat was forgotten, thank goodness.

We all sat on the front porch of the old house, fanning away flies, eating pie and visiting. We listened to Uncle Top spin yarn after yarn and tell dozens of old, worn-out country jokes and laughing loudly when he reached the punch line. I don't think anyone enjoyed Uncle Top's jokes more than Uncle Top. I listened intently as he talked of my paternal grandparents that I never knew, Shelby and Mary Holley. He would talk of some of the things that they all did together and the foolishness they had gotten into when they were all young. He told of ice cream suppers, box socials and musicals held at the community schoolhouse, and he talked of hard farm work and barely getting by. The Great Depression was still a vivid memory for him and Aunt Maggie. Shelby was his younger brother, and Mary was his sister-in-law. They were Dad's parents, and they had both passed away when Dad was 9 years old, leaving him and his three younger brothers orphaned.

The pleasant hum of front porch conversation lasted through the quiet Sunday afternoon, until finally Aunt Maggie said, "Naomer, before ya'll go home, I want you to see my garden; it's been real pretty this year, even with the long hot spell and all the dry weather. We've had more tomatoes and stick beans than we hardly know what to do with, and I have to can a bunch of butterbeans next week." While they were in the garden, talking of canning and preserving, Uncle Top was showing Dad and me his corn crop and tobacco patch.

"Clyde, it's been so hot and dry this year the crops ain't even going to pay for the seed we put in the ground."

"Yeah, we've been cutting corn stalks and collecting fodder (leaves), to feed the cows; not much nourishment in a mostly dried-up corn stalk, but I guess it's better than nothing," Dad said as he lit up his pipe.

"Daddy, can me and Butch go down to the creek?"

"Yeah, but don't fall in and watch for slick rocks and water moccasins."

Butch and I went to the little creek behind their house to look for tadpoles and minnows until Dad hollered, "Billy, come on, we've got to be heading for home in a few minutes."

Uncle Top and Aunt Maggie were joyous people, happy with their lot in life, their kids and with each other. Except for an old battery-powered radio, they had literally none of the material things in life that most of us want, but they had more of an abundance of the important things than some of us will ever have. They were thankful for what they had and never seemed to realize or be concerned about what they didn't have. They never seemed to miss the material things that they couldn't afford, and I never heard them complain. I guess we all could take a lesson from Uncle Top and Aunt Maggie.

END

LAS' PARKS AND THE MOLASSES FACTORY

Old-timers depended on molasses, not just as a tasty food and natural sweetener, but also in a variety of home remedies, such as mixing molasses with hot pepper to cure hiccups, or blending molasses with water to encourage roses to bloom. As for me, give me a frosty country morning, a warm kitchen and a stack of hot, buttered hoecakes smothered in molasses. A breakfast for kings; that's just my opinion of course.

In the 1940s, when I was still a young farm boy living in the rural South, Dad would plant a sorghum patch every spring. The patch was usually no more than 2 or 3 acres and primarily grown for livestock feed. He planted the round, buckshot-sized, brown seeds in bullet-straight rows using his old one-row, horse-drawn corn planter. This was much the same as you would plant corn, but the seeds were spaced much closer together. He utilized special sorghum seed distributor plates that temporarily replaced the regular corn planting plates in the bottom of the planter's seed hopper.

A few days after planting, the seeds sprouted, and tiny bright green leaves broke through the soil warmed by the spring sun. And if the early spring and summer rain cooperated, the plants would grow tall over the growing season, reaching maturity in the cool of late September. When fully grown, the leafy green cane would stand several feet taller than Dad, and he was 6 foot 2 inches tall.

As the cane began to ripen, Joe, my black shepherd dog, and I would make almost daily visits to the cane field. We walked up and down the rows; carefully avoiding the stiff, overlapping, sharp leaf blades that could make stinging cuts on exposed skin. I would search along the rows until I found the "perfect cane," whereupon I would break off the entire stalk at a joint closest to the ground. While Joe was chasing rabbits down the rows, I would strip the leaves (fodder) from the stalk and proceed to break the cane at each joint. One complete stalk would yield a number of pieces that were 10 to 12 inches long. *Sorghum cane has joints evenly spaced about 10 inches apart, and the stalk looks much like sugarcane or bamboo.*

Taking my collection of cane pieces, Joe and I would go to the nearest shade tree and park ourselves underneath. Using my bone-handle pocketknife, a gift from Pa, my granddad, I carefully peeled the hard outer layer away from the juicy pulp. I worked carefully, not wanting to cut myself on my knife or on the razor sharp edges of the cane's outer covering.

While Joe looked on, I would chew and spit the pale green pulp as long as the sweet-tasting sap lasted. I offered pieces to Joe, but he didn't seem too interested. He preferred the leftover biscuits and gravy from breakfast that Mother threw out the kitchen door each morning.

I quickly learned to limit my intake of the wonderful, sweet, greenish sap (juice), as too much would send a person on several daily trips to the outhouse.

SORGHUM FOR MOLASSES

In the early spring of 1944, Dad decided that he would plant an additional acre of sorghum, which would provide enough to feed the livestock during the hardest days of winter, and the extra would be enough to make us a batch of molasses. World War II was still raging, and sugar, syrup and other types of good sweeteners were scarce and seriously rationed, if any were available at all. The artificial sweetener, saccharine, was available, but the stuff was terrible as it left your mouth puckered and with a nasty, lingering aftertaste. I still remember my mother making "sweet" iced tea with that stuff.

Dad planted; the growing season was favorable; and the sorghum grew tall. The seasons changed, and the maple and hickory trees began to show the bright colors of late September. Dad, Joe and I would regularly visit the cane patch to check for maturity. Trustworthy analysis required that we chew a few pieces of cane on each visit to test the sweetness of the sap. When the juice was at its sweetest and the seeds were mature, the "molasses" cane was ready to be harvested and loaded on the wagon for the trip to *"Las' Parks' Molasses Factory."*

Finally, the long-awaited day came when Dad judged the cane sap to be at its peak of sweetness. "We'll get an early start after breakfast in the morning, and I believe that we can cut enough cane in the next day and a half for a load to take to the molasses mill." Early the next morning, chores finished, we were in the sorghum patch by 7:30 a.m. It was really cool, and a light frost covered the ground. All the sorghum harvesting tools were homemade and used by hand. Using a large knife that roughly resembled a dull machete, we carefully stripped the fodder from the cane as it stood in the field. After we had stripped all the fodder, we removed the seed heads using a homemade sorghum knife. The thin, sharp knife blade was bolted to the slotted end of an axe handle, the blade forming the short leg of an "L" shape. We put the fodder and seed heads into separate piles to haul to the barn later. We wasted nothing that we could use as feed for the livestock.

The second morning of cane harvesting, Dad and I were again in the field by 7:30 a.m. "We'll get the cane to Las' sorghum mill soon as we finish dinner today. Tomorrow morning we'll come back and load up the fodder and seed heads and haul them to the barn to help feed the livestock this winter," Dad said. Stripped of leaves and the seed heads removed, the sweet sap-laden cane was then cut close to the ground using the sorghum knife. As soon as it was all cut, Dad and I loaded the cane on the wagon for the trip to *"Las' Parks Molasses Factory."*

Before starting to cut cane, Dad warned, "Watch where you're going and don't step on one of them cane stobs, son; they got real sharp points that could go right through the bottom of your shoe and into your foot."

Dad and I finished loading all the cane, piling it high on the two-horse wagon. I helped as much as I could, but the load soon became too high for me to reach. Finally he said, "We're ready to go; let me boost you up to the top of the load. Now find yourself a spot in the middle of the load make a nest and stay there so you won't fall off. It's a long way down to the ground."

With me settled in reasonable comfort and safety on top of the load, Dad put his foot on the front wagon wheel hub and boosted himself up. He settled himself, and with the leather reins in hand, spoke to the team of mules, and we rolled out of the sorghum patch. We traveled down our lane to the gravel road that led to the sorghum mill, with the pleasant sound of gravel crunching under the iron rims of the wagon's wheels. I felt extremely self-important as I sat perched right behind Dad and high atop that load of cane. We had to travel west, less than 2 miles down the country road, to reach the mill. It was in a clearing, by the side of the road that led to the crossroads village of Delina, a mile farther on.

The 2-acre open area, where the mill operation was located, was bordered on the north by the road that we were traveling on. To the east was Delina creek, a winding stream of fresh water, gravel bars, huge rocks, deep pools and willow trees. A hillside full of tall scalybark hickory trees bordered the west side of the clearing. Farther to the south was a cow pasture with about a hundred of Avon Stone's grazing Holsteins. Avon ran a large milking operation. Across the creek from the clearing was a big cornfield. A few scattered scalybark trees grew in the clearing. It was a good year for nuts; they were almost as big as my fist, and the ground under the trees was covered with them.

His name was Las Parks, a black gentle giant of a man who stood over 6 foot 6. He was the proprietor of the Molasses Mill, or Factory, and the chief molasses maker. "Las'" was shortened from "Lasses," and that shortened from "Molasses," for those who were *educated* and chose to speak more properly. I was never sure if "Molasses" was his Christian name, as he came from a long line of molasses makers, or if it was given later because of his special talent for "'lasses making." I suspect that it was the latter.

Las' was ageless, with a wide, happy face, a crown of short, white nappy hair and a ready smile that revealed only an occasional tooth. He was a bit round from sampling his special product, and he was the blackest man that I ever knew. He was known miles around for his exceptional ability as a master maker of molasses. Las' even had his own special molasses-making uniform: an old sweat-stained, tattered brown felt hat, faded, worn overalls and a clean, starched white shirt. To complete the ensemble, he wore a loosely knotted tie with the end stuffed in the front of his shirt to keep it from getting caught on something. Las' was, after all, a professional businessman with an image to uphold.

Dad drove the horses and wagon off the main road down a slight, grassy embankment and into the grassless clearing; getting verbal and hand signal directions from Las' as to exactly where he should stop the wagon and position it for unloading the cane.

"Where do you want us, Las'?" Dad asked. "Come on in heah, mista Clyde, right over heah, thas right, jus' come on, come on, just a liddle bit mo, thas it, whoa! Thas real good right there. I see you got some mighty fine help sittin' on top of dat load of cane; how you, little Billy? Sho is good to see you folks. That's a real nice-looking load of cane, it'll make into some fine molasses, fine molasses, been a good year for cane," all said without Las' seeming to take a single breath.

I half slid, half fell off the wagon, using a back wheel and hub as a makeshift ladder, and immediately ran to the closest hickory tree and started picking hickory nuts off the ground. In a short time, I had filled the good-sized brown paper sack that I had stuffed into the bib pocket of my overalls before I left home that morning. Mother had reminded me that there were a lot of big hickory nut trees in and around the Molasses Factory. Hickory nuts are really hard to crack, but Mother's hickory nut pie was well worth the time and the mashed fingers caused from missing the said nut with a claw hammer.

While I was gathering nuts, Dad and Las' went about the business of unloading the cane and leaning it up against a wood rail. The rail, which was close to the mill, was made for that purpose. The cane had to be in just the right place to be easily accessible by the person feeding the mill.

Las' reached in the pocket of his overalls and pulled out his Barlow hawkbill pocketknife. With his thumb, he flipped open the single blade of the knife and cut a few small wedges of cane, chewing the pulp to sample the sap. "That juice sho' is sweet; this heah cane is goin' to make up into some mighty tasty 'lasses, Mista Clyde," said Las', grinning from ear to ear.

In the clearing stood all of the components of *The Molasses Factory*. On the outside perimeter but still close to the mill was the big cooking pan and alongside was a large stack of seasoned, split hickory wood. In the center of the clearing area stood the "squeezing" mill, which was about 5 feet off the ground, a heavy iron-and-steel contraption about as large in circumference as a number 2 washtub. The mill stood on four strong iron legs that were anchored in concrete so the mill was stationary.

Las' ran the mill on "one-mule power." One end of a long, straight locust pole was attached to a gear-drive shaft at the top of the mill. The other end of the pole was attached to the mule by means of a simple harness, trace chains and a single tree. The mule walked round and round in a circle turning the mill's rollers—crushing the cane and squeezing the juice into buckets. The person feeding cane into the mill's rollers had to duck the pole each time it came around, or get hit in the head with a painful reminder if he forgot. They usually got "beaned" once or twice before their memory greatly improved. Scary stories were told of careless molasses maker's hands and arms being pulled into a molasses mill's squeezing rollers and crushed. In addition, the combination of open flames and molten molasses was an ever-present danger. I seriously doubt that the FDA, OSHA or the EPA would have ever approved of Las's *"molasses factory"* operation if they had been around in those days. No government administration controlled molasses making back then, but Las' ran a clean operation.

Las' fed the sorghum cane into the mill's set of vertical and grooved, high-pressure rollers that rolled inward, crushing the stalks and squeezing out every drop of sap. The sap drained down into a large galvanized bucket that he placed on the ground beneath the mill. Several other buckets were stacked within easy reach, and as a full bucket was removed, he could quickly replace it with an empty one. The sap that filled the buckets was a watery, slightly sticky, pale green liquid that usually had quite a few bits and pieces of stalk and leaf parts floating on top.

As the mill turned, it spat the crushed stalk and pulp out on the opposite side from where Las' fed the cane, creating a growing pile of pulp, that could be hauled off by anyone looking for free livestock feed. If there were no takers and the pile grew too large,

Las' moved it to a site away from the mill and burned it, making a sweet-smelling bonfire.

The boiler pan looked similar to a long, heavy metal watering trough for horses. It was usually made by the local blacksmith specifically for molasses making. It was divided into a number of sections, with each section becoming progressively smaller, with the final and smallest section the finished molasses section. Las' molasses pan was approximately 12 feet long, 5 feet wide and 3 feet deep at its deepest point, and the pan held between 90 and 100 gallons of liquid.

A fire pit ran beneath the entire length of the pan, with a stovepipe at one end to carry away the smoke. The pit was filled with hot, even-burning hickory wood that burned to glowing coals during the entire cooking process. The heat had to be kept perfectly uniform beneath the pan. Years of use had turned the outside of the pan black and streaked from heat, smoke and soot.

Bucket after bucket of the thin, pale green liquid sap "squeezings" were collected and transported by hand from the mill to the pan, where it was strained clean by pouring it through a cotton feed sack or a large piece of muslin. The clean sap was strained into the first or "green sap" section of the boiling pan, which was the large "starter" section where the fresh sap cooked to an exact degree of consistency. Then a large, long-handled, wooden dipper, made for the purpose moved the liquid to the next section where the cooking continued, again to an exact degree of consistency, and so on— until the final molasses phase. This final phase was the most critical part of the entire process. Las' watched and controlled everything carefully from beginning to end.

Las' had a hired hand, a young black man named Claude whom he treated like a son. Claude's job was feeding the cane through the mill while Las' took care of the pan and the fine art of molasses making. Las' continually cautioned Claude "to be careful and pay attention to what you is doing." Las' had no children of his own and had started training Claude to take over the molasses-making business when Las' got too old to do the work. Las' even mentioned to Dad about how Claude was a real hard worker and how he was going to be an even better "lasses" maker than he was.

Having finished my hickory-nut gathering, I was already starting to get bored. I had explored the clearing and surrounding area as far as Dad would allow. I finally resorted to sitting on the ground, playing with a black-and-brown wooly worm to occupy my time.

Dad had sternly warned me to steer clear of the mule, the mill, the boiling molasses and the creek. He also warned me not to stray too far from the clearing. That didn't leave me a whole lot to do for entertainment. Seeing that I was bored, Las' came to my rescue, "Come on over heah, Billy; now don't get too close to dis old pan cause it's boiling hot. If it's all right with Mista Clyde, 'ol Las' goin show you how molasses is made." Las' looked at Dad who nodded his approval. "See dis heah first section? Das where the juice first go. Now dis last section, the one I'm stirring right now is jus about made molasses. Stand right over heah and watch 'ol Las'. Boiling sap foams, and I has to be constantly skimming it off the top with dis heah homemade wooden "skimmer." I made it with a long handle, so I wouldn't gets burned while I'm a-stirrin' and a-skimmin'. I put de skimmins in that barrel, and they is carted off by the farmers round here to be fed to their hogs. If I keep dem skimmins too long then dey ferments and if you feed that to dem hogs they gonna get fallin' down drunk and wobble all over de place." Las' drunk pig comment made Dad laugh and me giggle.

"Now as I stir, I is gonna dip and lift the paddle out of each section, to show you how the juice cooks down as it goes from one section to de next. See how the molasses makins' in each one has a different color and texture?"

The long step-by-step cooking process leads to a sudden and abrupt completion. Removing the finished molasses from the pan at just the right moment is critical to the success, or failure, of the entire molasses-making process. If you remove it from the pan a few minutes too soon, the molasses remains thin with a "green" taste and won't store well, plus the big problem is that it quickly runs off your hot, buttered breakfast biscuit and drips down your chin as you try to eat it.

The cane juice has to be stirred constantly, or it will stick and scorch, ruining the entire batch and becoming what is called "black strap," which is only suitable to sweeten livestock feed. Cook it too long, and it will cool thick and hard enough to bend spoon handles when you try to dig it out of the container.

If you remove it from the cooking pan at just the right time, the molasses cools to a translucent, greenish-golden, brown syrup that is easily spooned from a bucket or jar onto a breakfast biscuit. Good molasses is much thicker than syrup and will hold its place on a hot buttered biscuit or hoecake, giving you ample time to bite into its sweet, buttery goodness before it starts to run down your chin and over your fingers.

Las' didn't have any fancy high-tech tools for making molasses. No buttons, switches or gauges told him the exact moment when the molasses was finished. He just used his eyes, nose and the feel of his hands on the stirring and skimming paddle. He didn't need anything else, and he instinctively knew when the molasses had reached perfection. One could say that Las' had his own special scientific methodology. "You has to cook it until it gets frog eyes a bubbling up," Las' said, "and then you has got some mighty fine molasses, jus' then and not a second earlier or later." And sure enough, as the cane sap really started to thicken, the bubbles simmering on top began to look like frog eyes. "See Billy, see them frog eyes a poppin'; careful now don't get too close, 'ol Las' don't want you to gets burned."

Las' skimmed all the light mocha-colored foam off the "almost made" molasses and scraped it from his working paddle using a smaller paddle that he kept for the purpose. "Now Billy, when dat foam cool it make a real fine candy. Here, you can eats it right off the paddle."

While I ate the sweet chewy "foam" candy from the paddle, I continued to watch and listen to Las' and learn. "As I lifts the paddle, see how molasses streams off real slow, coming down to the size of a thin thread. These molasses are done, and they is about 1/10th the volume of the original juice."

"Look at dat greenish-golden color; now ain't that pretty with the sunlight shining thru?" he asked. "These 'lasses is ready to dip and pour into them little half-gallon buckets a sittin' right there next to you on the ground," Las' said. He worked quickly with a long-handled metal dipper. The latest batch of molasses was quickly dipped from the cooking pan and carefully poured into the shiny tin buckets that were the same as paint buckets, wire handle, tin top and all. Las' had plain white labels to stick on the sides of the buckets, on which he scribbled his name and address.

Las' didn't have a phone, but he was discovered by word of mouth, and his reputation spread far and wide anyway. Customers old and new found their way to Las' Parks' Molasses Factory.

I continued to watch the process with interest for quite a while, fascinated, until Las' finally said, "Now you knows more than mos' and you qualifies to be a real good lasses' maker; don't he, Mista Clyde?" My dad nodded his head in the affirmative, and I went in search of my wooly worm friend.

We didn't stay long enough that day to watch our own cane being made into molasses. We had to leave in time to get home and round up the cows for milking. Seems like most everything we did was centered around "milking time." Then again, Dad was never one to stand around for very long, watching someone else hard at work.

That year our sorghum patch produced 10, half-gallon buckets of Las' finest product. Las' took his usual one-eighth of the finished product as payment for his good work. Every molasses maker has his own way of judging when the molasses-making process is complete, and Las' was no exception. Some molasses makers look for the boiling bubbles to break the size of quarters on the surface of the boiling sorghum sap. Others withdraw the stir-paddle and look for the syrup-drip to thin out to the size of a hair. Some say it's a special color only they can see. Whatever the method, the call is made, and the molasses is now approximately one tenth the volume of the original juice.

Those wonderful molasses plus Mother's freshly churned butter and scratch biscuits helped to warm us on many cold mornings that following winter. For those who haven't had the good fortune to sample such a feast, they have my deepest sympathy.

END

FRANK AND
THE BUCKING CALF

Me and Frank Sullivan had spent the entire morning looking for something new and adventurous to get ourselves into. We didn't usually have any problem getting into mischief. The problem was getting ourselves out of trouble once we got into it. This morning seemed destined to be no exception. That's how Frank came to ride the half-grown, white-face Hereford calf.

When Frank was around, we seemed to always be doing stuff that got *me* in trouble, and I was the one that got my hide tanned. My folks thought Frank was a roughneck and a bad influence on me, and, as I look back on it, he probably was.

Frank was the oldest child of Lester and Virginia Sullivan. Frank's parents, two brothers and five sisters lived across the fields, less than a mile away from where my folks and I lived. Lester paid a few dollars a month rent on their three-room shotgun house with its sagging front porch and leaky roof.

I don't know how they all slept in that little unpainted shanty. They must have been stacked up like cordwood.

They were poorer than poor, living from hand to mouth. Lester got laid-off from his night-shift job at the stove foundry in a nearby town and had never been called back to work. He had been looking for a steady job ever since. The family barely existed on what little money Lester made, hiring out as a farm day laborer. He helped farmers in the community with their crops and cut bushes out of farm fence rows. The going wage for a hired-out farmhand was four dollars a day at best, and that didn't stretch very far, even in 1951. Virginia helped out as best she could, taking in washing, ironing and sewing. They did grow a big vegetable garden that helped sustain them through the summer, plus Virginia and the older girls canned a lot of vegetables and fruit from the fall harvest, shared by neighbors with farm orchards. Most of the neighbors helped out as much as they could, giving the family clothes that their own kids had outgrown. Occasionally the Sullivans found an anonymous envelope containing 10 one-dollar bills in their mailbox. They never found out who the secret benefactor was. Welfare and food stamps were available, but Lester was too proud to take any government handout. A few folks (we called them "big feeling") looked down their noses at the Sullivan family, calling them "poor white trash." They were doing the best they could at living, but life had given them a life of hard knocks for way too long. Kids at school made fun of Frank and his siblings for wearing clothes that some of them recognized as coming out of their own closets. Holding back the tears, he fought back because he didn't know what else to do, so he was labeled a bully. Frank was rough around the edges and that was a fact, but he had a good side and he was my friend.

My family was as poor as church mice, but Frank thought that we were rich.

Our rented tenant house was painted white; lace curtains were in the windows; and I even had my own room. It was off the kitchen and about the size of a closet. The pale green paint was peeling off the walls when we moved in, and mother papered it with wallpaper to keep the winter wind from whistling through the cracks, or so she said. We were poor financially, but we always had plenty to eat and clean clothes to wear.

Frank and I were about the same age. He was born in September of 1938, and I was born in November of 1939, the year that Hitler invaded Poland.

Because he was older, Frank thought he could tell me what to do and boss me around. Funny thing was that I would usually give in, not to his bossiness, but to his whining. I suppose I may never figure out why I tolerated Frank or considered him a friend. The world must have tilted slightly on its axis or something just as profound. Or maybe it was his adventurous spirit and the good heart at the core of his being.

———•———

Earlier that morning, for the first brave adventure of the day, we had climbed to the very top of the biggest sycamore tree that grew along the banks of Cane Creek. We pretended this was our lookout tree, and we were Indian warriors scouting for the evil white man. We could see for miles from the top of that tree, and if there had been any covered wagons for miles, we would have seen them. What we did see were grazing cattle, plowed fields, farmsteads and a red pickup leaving a trail of dust along the gravel road that ran by my house.

Seeing that there were no white pioneers about to attack us, we climbed down and out of the sycamore, and walked along the creek bank. We were looking for water moccasins sunning themselves as they lay coiled up on the big flat rocks that were exposed above the creek's water line. We found several, threw rocks at them, actually hitting a few, making them slip into the water and disappear. Frank's aim was better than mine, and he hit more of the critters than I did. But we both missed a lot more than we hit. The moccasins usually swam to a hole in the creek bank and quickly disappeared. We spotted one big 'ol moccasin stretched out on the trunk of a redbud tree that grew leaning out over the creek. We threw rocks until Frank finally hit the snake, and it dropped, with a plop, into the creek and swam away. We soon got tired of throwing rocks, and we ran out of snakes to torment anyway.

———•———

"Didja bring that sack of smoking tobacco and them cigarette papers with you?" asked Frank as we sat down on the creek bank, dangling our bare feet in the water while keeping a sharp eye out for any water moccasins that might be having thoughts about retaliation. I answered Frank by pulling a half-full sack of Country Gentleman and a folder of cigarette papers from the bib pocket of my overalls. I had collected the tobacco over time from Dad's almost empty tobacco sacks. I kept my tobacco stash hidden behind a rafter in the attic of our house. Dad would have skinned me alive if he had caught me stealing tobacco. I held the creased cigarette paper in my left hand just the way I had seen my dad, granddaddy and uncles do. I poured a generous amount of tobacco into the paper and passed the sack and papers over to Frank. Neither of us was practiced in the art of rolling your own cigarettes, and they looked sort of like tiny white submarines, fat in the middle and twisted at both ends to keep the loose tobacco from falling out.

I produced a pack of safety matches from my pocket. The cover advertised The Hi-Hat Café. I lit up my cigarette and passed the matchbook to Frank. We both leaned back, resting on our elbows, ready to relax and enjoy our rolled smokes. I took a big drag, tried to inhale and had a coughing spasm. We were just TOO COOL for words. Rolled too loosely, my cigarette came apart after a few drags, dropping its small fire coal on the front of my shirt, burning a hole and blistering a spot on my chest before I could jump up and knock it off. Dang it, now I had to figure out some excuse to explain to Mother the reason there was a hole burned in the front of my shirt. In other words, I had to come up with a believable lie.

Frank looked at me with a strange expression on his face. "You feelin' all right?" he asked. Ol' Frank was looking a little gray.

"Why'd you ask, don't I look all right?" I snapped.

"You look a little green, that's all."

"Well you look a little green yourself," I responded defensively, feeling like I was going to throw up at any moment."

"Them cigarettes done made us both sick; let's just lie back for a spell until the dizziness goes away and our stomachs stop doing flip-flops," Frank mumbled. He was trying hard to hold his breakfast down. This was our first adventure with cigarettes, and we couldn't even stand up, much less have walked a straight line if our lives had depended on it.

"What you gonna tell your Ma about that burned hole in your shirt?" he said, giggling.

"It ain't funny, Frank, but I think I got me an idea. There's a little pile of brush in the fencerow that runs along our sheep pasture. Dad and me have been aiming to burn it. I figure that now is a real good time to burn that old brush pile, and naturally a spark is going to pop out and burn this here hole in my shirt." I said, staring straight up at a sky that was still spinning.

"You could turn out to be a better liar than me if you keep working at it." Frank snickered.

We didn't have the sense to realize that our parents could smell the cigarette smoke on our clothes if we came within 30 feet. My folks never mentioned it, but a week later, sitting on the front porch at twilight, Dad passed me his pack of Chesterfields and strongly suggested that I join him in a smoke. He made me smoke the whole durn cigarette, and I got sick as a dog again. It was worse than when Frank and me were smoking down on the banks of the creek. That cured me of smoking for the next few years. I never asked Frank if his folks ever said anything.

A few days later Frank and I were stretched out on the grassy bank of Cane Creek staring up at the sky. "Is that old cable footbridge that your daddy built across the creek still there?" Frank asked absently, while we watched white puffy cloud *animals* glide across a summer sky.

"Sure, the cables are still there, but most of the boards to walk on are gone, and the rest are probably rotten by now." Cane Creek split our farm almost in half, and the dairy barn was across the creek from our house. Dad built the footbridge to get to the barn when the rains came and the water was too high to cross. Besides, he got tired of wading across the creek four times a day to do the milking, even when the water wasn't high. The bridge, we called it a *footlog*, was only a couple of hundred yards up the creek from where we were, and we were at the site in no time.

Four 1-inch diameter steel cables spanned the hundred feet from one side of the creek to the other. The cables were 30 feet or more above the creek bed, and just as I told Frank, most of the boards were missing, and the rest looked too rotten and dangerous to walk on. The cables were anchored to large trees that grew on opposite sides of the creek. The bottom two cables originally had the walking boards attached, using small "U" bolts. The boards were originally spaced 8 inches apart, but now many of the boards were missing. The footlog was maybe 3-feet wide, at the most. The top two cables were to hold on to, and you had to step carefully, even before the boards had rotted, as the space between allowed for a foot to slip through.

Naturally, Frank decided that I should be the one to go first. I must have been psychic, as I already knew what he was going to say. "Let's cross over to the other side, you go first."

"How come it's always me that has to do everything first? I ain't going to try to cross that old rotten bridge, Frank. If we accidentally fall through them rotten floorboards we'll hit them rocks below."

"Awww, come on, Billy, you've crossed this old bridge a thousand times before, but I ain't never. I should be more skerred than you."

"Well, doggone it, you're the one that wants to cross so bad, *you* go ahead," I said.

"Please Billy, I just want to watch and see how you do it, that's all," Frank whined. I knew that we'd be standing there arguing all day if I didn't cross the bridge first. Frank's whining had won again!

Using the lower cables to walk on, I crossed the bridge carefully and quickly, completely avoiding stepping on the boards. I knew without a doubt that the boards were too rotten to support my weight. Frank came behind me, nervously inching along on the cables. He gingerly tested the first board that he came to with his toe before he put any real weight on it. The board held.

More confident now, Frank tested the next board, again applying his foot before adding his full weight. "Frank, I told you them rotten boards won't hold your weight; walk on the cable…" CRRRAAAK, the board broke under Frank's weight, and one leg went all the way through. The broken boards fell end over end to the creek below. Frank had a narrow escape, but with a screaming panic, he managed to hang on to the swinging cable and to pull his leg back up.

"I can't go no further; I'm going back," Frank whined.

"Oh, come on Frank, stop whining; you're past the halfway point. The rest of the way is easy; just take one step at a time and walk on the cables like I keep telling you." It seemed to take forever, but I finally coaxed Frank across the 100-foot expanse of the creek. Reaching the other side, we sat a spell and caught our breath, enjoying our footlog victory. I was ready to re-cross the creek on the cables, but Frank had other ideas. He decided that we should skip the cables and wade the creek to get back across.

A remainder of what once was a well-worn path ran from the creek and the footlog across the pasture to my house. Walking along, I listened as Frank rattled on, and on, about how much fun crossing the footlog had been and what our next adventure for today might be. As we walked past our small herd of half-grown Hereford calves, I said, "I think we've had enough of your so-called *brave adventures* for one day, Frank. Let's get that stack of Super Man and Captain Marvel comic books that's under my bed and read them under the shade tree in the back yard." I got no response from Frank, so I had to assume that the comic book idea didn't hit his "adventure button."

"I got an idea; that brush pile that I'm going to burn is down that fence row a short way; let's go burn it while we're this close."

We turned from the path and walked along the nearby fence line to the small pile of dry brush that was to be my alibi for the burned hole in my shirt. I gathered a few hands full of dry sage grass and stuck it under the corner of the pile of brush, lighting it with a match from the matchbook that Frank carried in his overalls pocket. We watched quietly as the fire quickly consumed the brush. We stayed long enough to make sure that the fire wouldn't spread before returning to the path and continuing on toward the house.

Frank and I were both quiet for a few minutes before Frank, totally ignoring my comic book suggestion, said, "You ever rode one of them whiteface calves we passed back there?"

I could almost hear the wheels turning and clanking in his head. "No I ain't, you can't ride a durn calf," I said.

"Why not?" I'll bet you could train one of them half-grown calves to be rode just like a pony."

"Frank, we are NOT going to ride one of them Hereford calves; besides my Dad would have a fit. He's going to market with them in a couple of weeks, and if we got caught running one pound off any one of them, he'll tan my hide. I get more than my share of whoopings because of you, anyhow."

"Oh, come on Billy, it'll be fun," Frank kept on talking; actually it was more like his usual whining and wheedling, but even more so.

I finally gave in as usual just to shut him up. I wouldn't have admitted it to Frank in a million, make that two million years, but I was a little curious myself as to whether he could stay on a calf for the eight-second rodeo rider's count. We reached the barn, and I grabbed a feed bucket hanging from its nail in the hall and poured a little shelled corn into it from the tow sack in the feed room. Just enough corn to rattle in the bottom of the bucket with a noise identifiable as "food" to the calves. Sure enough, as soon as they heard the sound, they came running like their tails were afire.

I told Frank to hide out in the feed room while I coaxed one of the calves into a handy and empty stable. Frank got a rope halter down from its peg in the feed room. Dad kept all of his plow and wagon harnesses, ropes, saddles, bridles, halters and such hanging on pegs in the feed room. I was in the stable with the now uneasy steer, and Frank passed the halter to me through a crack in the stable door. The calf was halter-broke, so there was no problem getting it on his head, then leading our "victim" out of the stable. Once the calf, Frank and I were out of the stable and into the barn hall, Frank said, "Okay, I'll hold the halter rope. You climb on the calf. Once you get settled, I'll hand you the rope."

"Oh no you don't, Frank, nope, not this time; this was your bright idea to ride this danged calf, and I ain't a-fixin' to climb on his back and get my neck broke." Try as he might, using all of his best whining and wheedling arsenal, this time I didn't give in. What Frank didn't know and I didn't bother to tell him was that I had tried to ride the calf a couple of mornings before and got thrown a-winding.

Finally, curiosity got the best of ol' Frank. He started to climb aboard the calf, and that was more than the jittery critter could stand. The calf stood stone still for a couple of seconds, then dropped his head and commenced to pull back hard on the halter lead, but I managed to hold on. Frank wrapped his legs around the calf's round barrel belly as best he could and grabbed himself a double handful of calf hair and hide and hung on. The halter lead rope was dragging the ground.

First off, the calf tried to brush Frank off his back by running along the barn hall wall, but Frank managed to hang on. Then the calf really got walleyed, jerked his head to the side and started to buck and frog jump. He jerked the lead rope completely out of my hands, giving me a rope burn in the process. Free, the calf started to jump sideways and do a windmill spin. "Ride 'em, Frank!" I yelled through spasms of laughter. That calf would have made any prize rodeo bull proud. Frank was hollering "WOAHHH,

WOAHHHHH" and hanging on to that calf with a death grip. No professional bull rider in a championship rodeo could have done a better job of riding that calf than ol' Frank. They probably wouldn't have screamed near as much, though. Frank hung on, even though the calf's loose hide wasn't much for gripping. Bawling, the calf left the hall and headed for the barn lot, bucking and jumping every step of the way. Out into the open pasture, he bucked right through a blackberry briar patch and too close to a thorny hedge-apple tree. Frank was still hanging on, but the calf's hide was really loose, and the more the calf bucked, jumped and twisted, the more Frank slid sideways. The more he slid, the louder his screams of "WOAHHHHH." The more he screamed, the harder I laughed. Now Frank was totally sideways and was headed south, head first.

"Hang on to him Frank, you done got him rode." I yelled, but I think Frank was too busy to pay me any attention at that moment.

"Woahhhhhhhhhh you dern fool calf, WOAHHHHH SOMBICH," Frank yelled just before he slid completely off and hit the hard-packed ground, head first. The calf, still bucking and jumping and still wearing the halter, headed out to the far side pasture, joining the rest of the herd. I knew that I would have some serious explaining (lying) to do when Dad came in from plowing corn and saw the calf in the pasture with the halter still on his head and dragging the lead rope.

Frank lay on the ground, not moving. "Frank, Frank, are you all right?" I yelled, as I ran to where he was lying, thinking that he might be dead. Frank, moaning, was covered in scratches from head to toe, and his clothes were ripped from his trip through the briar patch and sideswiping the hedge apple bush.

"Knocked the breath out of me," he managed to wheeze out in a whisper.

"Anything get broken Frank?" I asked, suppressing a giggle that finally escaped. "Frank you sure were a funny sight riding that calf."

"Ain't nothing funny, I durn near killed myself; I think I might have broke something, I ain't checked everything yet. All you can do is laugh. Some friend you are!"

"Well, for once I got one over on you, Frank. It looks like you're gonna live; come on up to the house, and we'll clean you up and put some iodine on those scratches, and maybe band-aid the worst ones. 'Course you'll have to get some of that dirt and cow manure off before Mother will let you anywhere close to the inside of her clean house. Probably be best to wash some of it off in the spring branch behind the barn. I think a slice of Mother's lemon pie might cure some of the pain and embarrassment that you might be feeling. I figure that you have to be feeling real embarrassed about now, seeing as how you couldn't stay on that little old calf."

On the path from the barn to the house, Frank didn't say a word; he just glared at me and sulked as he limped along. He was almost through with his second slice of pie before he forgot his ill-fated "bull-riding" experience and started talking again. Mother babied Frank, allowing as he might have been killed and of course, Frank ate up the attention.

"Son, you've burned a hole in your shirt. How did you manage to do that?" she asked.

"We stopped by and burned that brush pile me and Daddy's been meaning to burn, and a spark popped out and burned my shirt and blistered a spot on my chest, too. I got no sympathy from Mother at all. All I got was, "you need to be more careful son. You shouldn't have burned the brush without your daddy, the fire could have gotten out of control."

"We were real careful, Mother; honest we were." I gave Frank a sideways glance, daring him to say a word about the hole in my shirt.

Then, in true Frank fashion, he started to brag about how long he had stayed on the calf before he got thrown off. Good ol' Frank. You'd have thought he was a champion bull rider to hear him brag. "We done had us some serious adventure today, Billy." I looked sideways at Frank, grunted, and let it go at that.

Late that afternoon Frank had gone home, and I was at the barn finishing chores and nervously waiting on Dad to come in from plowing. I had decided that honesty was the best policy, so I took a deep breath soon as he arrived and told him the whole story, ready for the worst. Instead of getting the expected whooping with a plow line, Dad started laughing and laughed so hard he almost lost his breath.

"I'd have loved to seen Frank trying to ride that calf. I guess your ol' buddy Frank got just about what he deserved from that calf. What goes round comes round. He's shore done his share of getting you in trouble, ain't he?" Son, did you try to ride that calf?

Just another summer day of farm fun and adventure in 1951.

END

MILKING TIME

My summer-browned bare feet stirred up small puffs of dust as I ran along the winding, timeworn and rutted cow path that ran from our barn across the pasture. It hadn't rained in weeks, and the dirt that made up the path had been hoof trampled and traveled over until its dust was ground fine as talcum powder. Wearing no shoes made me feel so light that it was almost as if I were flying, and I sailed right over the fresh cow patties and carefully negotiated the bull nettles' thorns, sharp rocks and wild blackberry vines. Bull nettles that were determined to grow in the hard path were ready to leave their sharp thorns in my toes if I made a misstep. Blackberry vines grew in abundant patches along the path and seemed eager to reach out to snag my clothes and scratch my skin with their sharp thorns. The long dry spell had ensured that there would be no vines filled with juicy blackberries to pick this year.

Joe, my big black dog of questionable pedigree, cut a zigzag path across the pasture, close behind his current rabbit interest. Joe always gave rabbits a good run, but I never saw him actually catch one. It seemed to be more of a fun game for dog and rabbit. The rabbit always seemed to get to the safety of a briar patch just before Joe could catch him. Joe was a big dog with a shiny coat that was long, black and wavy. Patches on his chest, belly and all four feet were snow white. Part of his muzzle was rust-brown, and one ear was up while one was down. The mismatched ears gave Joe the look of always questioning whatever was said to him. He never missed an opportunity to chase a rabbit or a squirrel or stick his head into every groundhog hole that he encountered along the edge of the woods. And he never missed catching the biscuit that Mother tossed out the back kitchen door every morning after our breakfast was over.

One morning as I was watching Joe chase a rabbit through the sage grass, I wasn't paying attention to where I was going and almost stepped on a big black racer snake that was inching its way lazily across the path. I took immediate flight and sailed completely over the critter with plenty of air space to spare. I don't think he ever knew that I was there.

The sun was dropping in the west, turning the late afternoon sky red-orange and purple. The few scattered clouds were outlined in pure gold. The herd of Jersey and mixed-breed dairy cows were slowly grazing their way toward the barn as usual this time of the late afternoon. A few strays in the far corner of the pasture held back from the rest of the herd, insisting on snagging that last mouthful or two of grass, I suppose, or maybe they were just being ornery. I sent Joe to round up the stragglers that were part of the herd that was supposed to be milked. A few members of the herd were "dry," which meant the cows were due to calve in a few weeks, and we had stopped milking them. Joe was really smart and knew which cows were supposed to go to the barn and which stayed in the pasture. He had the herding instincts of an English shepherd, and I suspect that one was present somewhere in his ancestry. A few nips on the cattle's back heels from old Joe quickly persuaded the strays of their errant ways and to move along at a brisk trot.

Rounding up our herd of 15 cows for their twice-a-day milking was more of a daily adventure for me to enjoy than a chore. I always found something new to discover in the big cow pasture that rose up the hill behind our old barn: interesting "fossil" rocks and occasional arrowheads to fill my pockets; and bugs, worms and butterflies to observe, plus all sorts of wild critters; foxes, rabbits, squirrels and 'possums for Joe to chase.

As Joe and I drove the herd down the path and got closer to the barn, Mother was waiting patiently by the open door to the milk shed. She helped drive the cows into the shed, which was attached to the side of the main barn and ran its full length. She had already distributed feed in the long concrete trough in the milk shed. The feed was stored in a 55-gallon metal drum that long ago had been used to ship oil. We gave each cow a half-gallon of feed, measured in an old tin coffee can. The cows were eager for their evening feed ration and filed through the open door in a quick but orderly fashion. We fed them morning and evening at milking time. Finding their spot in the long row of waiting wooden stanchions, they poked their heads through to reach and eat the crushed corn and cottonseed meal that we mixed with blackstrap molasses. We called this concoction *sweet feed,* and the cows loved it. The wooden stanchions were designed so that they could all be closed at the same time by pulling one of the wooden levers, located at each end of the row of stanchions, locking the cow's heads, so they couldn't run off while we were doing the milking. I never did quite understand how the cows knew to go to *their spot* every time, but they did, and I suppose it was the twice-daily routine.

We milked *by hand* for years before we finally graduated up to mechanical milking machines. Our pre-machine *milking equipment* consisted of a homemade, three-legged wooden milking stool to sit on, a stainless steel milk bucket that held 2 gallons of milk, and our two hands. You always approached the right side of the cow; sat on the stool that was usually no more than 12 to 14 inches off the ground, then carefully positioned the bucket directly under the cow's udder. Then, with a fair amount of dexterity, plus training, experience and the use of both hands, you squeezed two teats at a time until the udders were empty and every last drop of milk was in the bucket. This process did take a certain amount of practice to become proficient in hitting the bucket with each squirt of milk. As each cow was *milked,* the buckets' contents were emptied into a stainless steel milk *strainer* that sat atop an open milk can. A disposable cotton pad in the bottom of the strainer filtered out any impurities that might have found their way into the bucket.

The steel milk can, which held 10 gallons of milk, had bright red identifying numbers loosely painted on the shoulders of the can and on the can's lid. The numbers told the milk truck driver and the milk plant what farm the milk cans belonged to, so the cans could be correctly returned each day. The accounting depart-ment of the milk plant also used the identifying number to know what to pay the farmer for the milk sold.

After all the cows were milked and the milk strained, a clean, beat-up aluminum dipper, that had former life in a kitchen water bucket, was used to dip milk from the milk can into a 1-gallon glass jug that once contained vinegar. On the way to the house after milking and finishing barn chores, we would drop off the milk jug at the spring branch that ran a few yards from our back door. We placed the jug of fresh milk up to its neck in the fresh spring water to cool. This served as our household daily supply of milk for drinking and cooking. Mother skimmed the thick, rich cream off the top of the milk for butter churning.

In summer, the full cans of milk were picked up morning and evening by a milk truck, which transported the milk to be processed at the Marshall County Creamery in the nearby town of Lewisburg. During the fall and winter months, the truck picked up the milk cans once each day, usually in the morning.

The whole milking process sounds simple, easy and pain-less; doesn't it? You just move from cow to cow, sitting on your wooden stool, milking each cow until the entire chore is complete, a process that doesn't take more than 15 minutes per cow. Think again! You've never lived the dairy barn experience until you've been slapped hard, up-side the head, with the switch of a cow's tail filled and matted with cockleburs in the fall of the year. Or chunks of ice and frozen mud or who knows what, during the winter. Then there's the cow that decides to sock one of her back hoofs in the milk bucket just as you've squeezed the last squirt of milk into a full bucket. Of course, there's always the fresh cow patties that they decide to drop while you're milking. These are some of the more unpleasant parts of the old-fashioned hand-milking process.

When milking was complete and the cows were turned out of the milk shed and into the night pasture, it was time to carefully wash and sanitize the milk buckets and strainers. The last chore, and the one that I hated the most, was to clean out and wash down the milk shed. The fresh manure that was inevitably left behind was scooped up with manure forks and scoops and added to the growing pile at the back of the barn. Over fall and winter, the manure would compost and become rich fertilizer to spread on next spring's vegetable garden, farm fields and pastures.

Obviously, the way we milked cows would not be considered a very sanitary or healthy process by today's standards, I know, but I grew up drinking whole milk, buttermilk and eating fresh-churned butter. I never knew anyone to get sick from drinking farm fresh milk except my mother, and she was lactose-intolerant. One of my favorite suppers was a glass of whole milk or buttermilk with a big wedge of fresh-baked, hot cornbread crumbled in it. And for breakfast on a cold winter morning, freshly churned homemade butter and molasses sure tasted good on a skillet-fried spoon biscuit.

Do you suppose that you would survive the experience of drinking a tall cool glass of milk if it was processed this way today?

Times change. Our state and federal government took more and more interest in how milk was collected and processed at the dairy barn. Inspectors checked the barns on a regular basis, made a few notes and determined whether or not a farmer could sell the milk that he produced. Many farmers gave up trying to sell milk and sold off their entire dairy herds and went out of the milk business permanently. They couldn't afford the cost of building and then keeping up with all the rules and regulations of operating a Grade A parlor-type milk barn. It was an unfortunate situation since most of the farmers depended on the milk check as one of the few regular monthly cash incomes that they could depend on. Government rules and regulations changed almost month to month like most government rules. The changing rules left most farmers who sold milk confused and wondering what the government inspectors might decide to change next.

No doubt the government was trying to do the right thing in closing down the milk sheds in favor of the more sanitary Grade A milking parlors. Their intention was to make sure that the public was supplied with good, clean, wholesome pasteurized milk. This type of continuing government intrusion is the price we pay for *progress*, I suppose.

A few of the more prosperous farmers in our community built fancy *government-approved* Grade A milking parlors with concrete floors and stainless steel equipment. Some dairy farmers had a herd of as many as 150 cows. Milk was collected with electric milking machines, filtered and piped through glass pipelines directly into large stainless steel tanks that were kept at a consistent degree of temperature as required by government standards. The milk was then pumped from the dairy holding tanks into the stainless steel tanks of milk trucks to be delivered to Grade A milk plants.

For a few more years, Dad and a few of his neighbors were *milk shed* holdouts and sold milk the same way they always had. Even after our can-hauling milk truck stopped operating, Dad would load the full cans of milk in his old pickup truck and haul them 13 miles to the creamery in Lewisburg. The creamery made *Wisconsin Hoop Cheese;* that's right, Wisconsin Hoop, and for a time, continued to accept farm milk in cans. Finally, the government again intervened, and the creamery could no longer accept milk in 10-gallon stainless steel cans.

Today, long years later, I have to consider that if the raw milk and the butter that my family and my neighbors consumed every day was so contaminated and germ-ridden, how did we and all of the people that we knew survive and thrive on it?

END

A DELINA
SATURDAY AFTERNOON

It was just past the noon hour on a Saturday, the middle of August 1944. The heat and powdery mocha-colored dust of the "dog days of summer" lay like a thick, hazy mantle over the hills and valleys of Southern Middle Tennessee. Not a leaf stirred. It was as if everything and everyone in our small rural universe were dozing. The old folks sat in rocking chairs on their front porches, armed with a cardboard fan from Beasley's Funeral Home in one hand and a flyswatter in the other. Their only movement was slow rocking and an occasional whack at an irritating fly that seemed bent on aggravation and staying just out of reach of the swatter. Conversation was mostly non-existent, as folks weren't inclined to put forth enough energy to start, much less continue any sort of participation, verbal or otherwise. The high-pitched and constant hum of summer insects seemed to emphasize the dullness and the heat. It was as though the heat itself was creating the hum. This was the summer of my fifth birthday.

If you were a farm family in the south, most everything slowed to a standstill at noon on Saturday, and for a little while, work was set aside. Saturday afternoons were cherished almost as much as Sundays, the official day of rest. It was a brief time-out from the dust, sweat and blisters of backbreaking farm work. Folks took their weekly bath and put on clean clothes in preparation for the once-a-week trip to the country store to buy groceries and supplies. The menfolks harnessed the team and hitched them to the wagon or the buggy. If you were well off enough to own a family car, one that would still run, it would have been freshly washed and shined up. Whatever the family transportation, it was usually loaded up with chickens, eggs, side meat and maybe a couple of cured 'possum and polecat hides, all collected to trade out for groceries or other needed staples. If there was a more costly need like a plow or outfitting the family in new shoes, a cured country ham might be added to the bartering mix.

After breakfast on this particular Saturday morning and in preparation for our trip to Delina, Mother had kept the wood-burning kitchen stove fired up. The cast iron teakettle was sitting on the back eye of the stove, full of steaming hot water for our weekly baths. My turn at the hot bathwater came first in the old No. 2 galvanized washtub. Mother had placed the tub in the shade of the huge old oak tree in the backyard. I stripped naked and timidly stuck a toe in the water. It was hot but bearable. Since no neighbors were within "seeing distance" of our house, I didn't have a problem with stripping down. Her homemade lye soap, lathered up, made quick work of my morning's accumulation of dirt and grime. Plus, with the addition of Mother's determined scrubbing, it felt like the loss of a couple of layers of skin. She scrubbed my ears and neck until they were beet red; my blonde wispy hair was wet-combed and plastered to my head.

While Mother helped me with my clothes, Dad stripped and hopped in the tub for his weekly scrub down. Mother had had her bath the night before in the kitchen, so she could enjoy some privacy. Now she smelled good, of face powder and lavender. Dressed, ready to go in my homemade overalls and a colorful shirt made from a sack that once held cow feed, I was warned not to get dirty and actually managed to keep the dirt down to a few smudges here and there.

Mother looked pretty in her homemade print dress, the cream-colored one with the little pink flowers and white collar and cuffs. Dad was decked out in his white Panama hat, starched and ironed overalls, tan work shirt and "Sunday shoes." He must have had those shoes for more than 20 years and they were always shined. *Starched* was the operational word at our house, because Mother starched and ironed everything that went through the wash, and I do mean everything. Have you ever worn a pair of heavily starched drawers? I can tell you from experience that it's kind of like wearing sandpaper.

We may have been poor by anything financial, but we were proud and clean. And we always had wonderful food and full bellies, thanks to Mother's summer canning, and a smokehouse filled with meat from the previous winter's hog killing.

World War II was raging, and everything was rationed...gas, tires, sugar, coffee, lard, tea, cigarettes...everything. Most of our neighbors were forced to put their cars and pickup trucks up on concrete blocks, as no rubber for tires was available. All the rubber was being used in the war. Few engine repairs could be done, as tin, iron and steel all went to the war effort, too. Folks resorted to riding horseback, traveling in horse-drawn wagons, and buggies... or they walked. You had to sign up to get U.S. government-issued stamps for staples, based on each individual family's need. For instance, you might be issued 10 stamps for 10 pounds of sugar for a month. If you ran out of stamps and sugar before the month was up...you had to do without until you again became eligible for sugar stamps. Dad was more frugal than most of our neighbors with our gas stamps, so we always had a little gas in the tank of our old Model A Ford pickup. The truck was reserved for emergencies and seldom driven.

Baths complete, dressed in clean clothes and barter items collected, we all climbed aboard the black horse-drawn buggy. Mother and Dad rode up front in the wide seat, and I was scrunched up in the back on the tiny single seat. Dad lifted the reins, spoke gently to Blackie, the buggy mare, and away we went down the dusty, winding lane. The lane led to the main county road a half-mile from our old house. The bright red, high-spoke wheels spun merrily in the early afternoon sun as they crunched the road gravel and kicked up small puffs of dust.

We passed the orchard where our small flock of 20 sheep rested in the shade of the apple and peach trees. Too lazy to get up, one old ewe stretched her neck to reach for a windfall apple to munch on. Riding in the buggy was fun as you had plenty of time to take in the sights, sounds and smells along the way. The smell of honeysuckle filled the air. Milk cows stopped grazing, lifted their heads and stared with curiosity as we passed by. A couple of young Jersey calves stood in the lane right in front of us, staring wide-eyed until we got too close for comfort. At the last minute, they did a bucking jump and ran to the open pasture, with tails curled over their backs. They stopped at a safe distance to stare once more.

The weeds, grass and wildflowers alongside the road were covered with a layer of dust. Big yellow and black butterflies fluttered from one orange butterfly weed to the next. In the cornfields next to the road, the stalks were tall, and bright green with ears already too hard for cooking. Fresh corn roasted in the oven was one of my favorite things to eat. Golden wheat, barley and oats, soon to be ready for harvest, made gentle green-gold waves in the hot summer breeze. Tall tulip poplars turned the undersides of their leaves to the sky begging for rain. "Better not stay too long in Delina," Dad mumbled. "From the looks of them leaves, it's gonna rain before long, maybe even late today. Sure could use a little rain; I just hope it doesn't come with a big wind as that would flatten the grain, for certain. And that would really hurt us all financially if we lost our crop of small grain."

Making pleasant small talk, Mother clung tightly to the large willow basket in her lap. The basket was lined with one of her clean red-and-white checked dishtowels and filled with three dozen fresh brown hen eggs that I had gathered from the hen nests the night before.

We rode past the grove of giant scaly-bark hickory nut trees, and on past the patches of persimmon and sumac bushes that grew near the end of our lane. Dad slapped the reins along Blackie's back. She snorted and picked up the pace as she turned from our lane onto the winding gravel road that led to Delina. This small country crossroad village was the gathering place for all the families in the community. It was just four miles from the old Elwood MacAfee Farm where we lived and where Dad sharecropped on the halves. "On the halves" meant that Elwood supplied the land, and Dad provided the labor. They split any of the actual seed and fertilizer costs, and profits if there were any.

We rounded a curve in the road and then crossed the old wooden bridge that spanned Delina Creek. As we passed by the white clapboard Wiser house on the right, we all waved to Annabelle Wiser as she hung the family wash on the line. She waved back and called out a muffled greeting around a mouthful of wooden clothespins. White sheets, bright flowery dresses and her husband Bobby Joe's gray drawers all flapped in the breeze. "Need anything from Delina?" asked Mom. "Well, you could bring me some bluing and a box of Rinso." Bluing was round, about the size of a marble and when added to rinse water it made the white clothes appear brighter. Rinso was a soap powder that was really popular with housewives at the time. Rinso sponsored some of the early radio soap operas. "I'll pay you for it when you come back by." My mother and Annabelle had been friends since grammar school.

Delina was our "community shopping center." It was a mix of four competing grocery/mercantile stores, a service station and one blacksmith shop owned by Walt Bradford. Walt was a giant of a man with a friendly attitude who always seemed to have a layer of black axle grease on his coveralls, charcoal smudges on his face and hands, and a big smile.

When we arrived, Delina was a hot swirling, dust cloud that covered everything. It choked you, filled your nostrils and stung your eyes. The buildings were barely more than silhouettes. The dust came from old cars, horses pulling work wagons, black buggies with red or yellow wheels, kids and assorted dogs...hounds mostly. We rode right into the middle of the dusty chaos. Dad found an open spot at the hitch rail in front of Huey Bigham's store and climbed down from the buggy to tie up Blackie. Then he helped Mother down with her basket of eggs. I had already scrambled down off the back of the buggy, ready for any big adventure that might unfold.

The stores offered everything from groceries and livestock feed to clothes, gasoline and plow points. The store buildings were mostly white or graying clapboard with tall false fronts that displayed the owner's name in big letters. Letters that once were black or bright red, but time and the elements had faded the paint until the lettering on most of the stores had almost disappeared. The exterior clapboard walls were decorated with brightly printed metal signs advertising Prince Albert Smoking Tobacco, NEHI Grape, Coca-Cola, Garrett Sweet Snuff, Calumet Baking Powder and dozens of other products.

The store's chipped and time-stained concrete porches held an assortment of nail kegs, wooden soft drink cases and benches where the men would sit, smoke hand-rolled cigarettes and drink *CoColas*, the generic term used for any soft drink. This was the time for relaxation and time to spend swapping farming and hunting stories. They had mostly good-natured banter, talked politics and the war in Europe, while their whittling contributed to a growing pile of fragrant cedar wood shavings. The war was a somber topic and usually got the greatest conversational attention, as most of the neighbors had at least one family member in the service and some had already lost loved ones in battle.

The women caught up on the latest gossip as they shopped; they shared what they had heard eavesdropping on the telephone party line. They traded eggs, homegrown produce, money and ration stamps for the few basics that were usually needed, things like sugar, salt, rice, tea, and chicory coffee. Real coffee was almost non-existent as it too was going to the war effort. For a special breakfast treat, a box of Post Toasties and a half-gallon glass jug of Karo Syrup might be added to the list.

We and nearly all the neighboring farm families planted big vegetable gardens and did a lot of canning during the summer and early fall. We also grew our own chickens that supplied us with eggs and Sunday fried chicken. In addition, we ate homegrown pork and beef, so our grocery needs were usually small.

I can remember Mother "putting up" hundreds of quart glass Mason jars filled with vegetables, fruits, pickles, green tomato and corn relish. The shelves were filled with rows and rows of bright colorful jars. Canning was a social event for the women of the community as they helped each other prepare food for the winter. Dad often said that he felt sorry "for them city folks that had to live out of a brown paper sack." He thought everyone should work hard and try their best to be self-sufficient.

A big game of horseshoes was always going on in the pasture just behind Bigham's General Store. Mostly the older men played, and the competition was intense with lots of ribbing, cussing, laughter and tobacco-spitting. You would have thought those games of horseshoes were the equivalent of the World Series with all the hollering, cussing and side bets going on.

Out behind Walt Bradford's blacksmith shop was the local softball field. The teams were mostly made up of the local teenage boys and girls, but some of the adult men and women played, too. The field doubled as a cow pasture for Bubby Downing's cows, and if you played ball you quickly learned to dodge the cow patties, particularly the fresh ones, as you slid into home plate. The folks around Delina took their softball games seriously, too, so seriously in fact that more than once the game was cut short by a fistfight between rival teams.

Little kids played tag or Red Rover, chased each other, and were generally underfoot and in the way of the older folks. Since

I was the shy, quiet type, and under the constant "evil eye" of Dad, there always seemed to be the promise of a "whooping," so I stayed close by one or the other of my parents, and mostly kept my mouth shut as I watched the other kids play games.

On this particular Saturday afternoon, the "routine" was interrupted by a new noise. Everything stopped, and all eyes turned skyward. A small, bright yellow, single-engine plane buzzed low over Delina, scaring the daylights out of the horses, thereby creating even more of a dust cloud chaos. After a couple more low passes, the Piper Cub made a final approach and expertly side-slipped into Hubert Doggett's big cow pasture on the outskirts of Delina. Somehow, as he came in for a landing, the pilot managed to miss all of the cows in the big herd of grazing Holsteins. The pilot climbed out of the plane, pulling off his leather flying cap and goggles as he walked over and introduced himself to the closest folks. He said that his name was Hoop Stevens, and that he had flown over from Fayetteville, a small town some 30 miles south/southeast of Delina. He further explained that he was on his way to Columbia, Tennessee, 50 miles or so northwest. As he was flying over, he saw the dust below and all the activity and was curious as to what the ruckus was all about. One old farmer, known to be grouchy, complained about how the flyover buzz scared his horses. "They durn near run off when you buzzed us," he groused, spitting streams of tobacco juice. His disposition brightened considerably and his mood was soothed when Hoop apologized and then strode over to Lane's store where he bought a couple of RC Colas and Moon Pies for the old man and himself.

Hoop spent time visiting and giving the kids, the curious adults and some of the older folks time to look over the aircraft from one end to the other before he took off. Not many Delina folks had ever seen an airplane up close. Finally, the visit over, he leaned into the cockpit and tinkered for a moment with the controls. Then, walking to the front of the plane, he gave the propeller a couple of hard pulls, and the plane's engine sputtered to life. "I don't think I have enough room in this pasture to take off in the normal way. Would a couple of you strong young fellers be kind enough to get behind the wing on each side of the plane and hold on to it? I'll rev up the engine and you can release your grip at my signal. I think I can lift off before I run into those trees over yonder on the other side of the pasture."

Waving to the crowd, he climbed into the cockpit, latched the door and revved up the engine while the men held on to the wing. Throttle open, engine humming and the little plane vibrating, he signaled for the men to release the wing. He taxied across the pasture, quickly picking up speed until he was airborne, barely missing the trees at the pasture's edge. As he took to the air, he circled a couple of times, then flew directly over Delina, rocking his wings in a final salute as he continued on his journey. Folks watched until the little plane was a tiny yellow speck, fading in the distance until it was completely out of sight.

I guess every community of any size at all could lay claim to their own town drunks, and Delina was no different in that respect. My good-natured Uncle Thurston and his sidekick Paul Hawkins could be expected to show up every Saturday afternoon, drunker than skunks on moonshine bought from Sam Mulenkamp, the local bootlegger.

Bright and early on most Saturday mornings, Thurston and Paul would drop by the bootlegger's for a quart fruit jar filled with the clear, fiery liquid. With the jug and fishing tackle in hand, they would head for one of their favorite fishing spots under the willows along the banks of Delina Creek. After a morning of a lot more drinking than fishing, they would come roaring into Delina in the middle of the afternoon. They made sure to create a huge cloud of dust with Thurston at the wheel of whichever one's rattle-trap car that would start and run that day. The commotion always sent chickens, dogs, kids and horses scurrying in every direction. With everyone's attention directed at them…they would slowly open the car doors and get out. Weaving back and forth, they would hold up the string of the morning's catch, usually 8 or 10 tiny bream and bluegill, just barely large enough to pan fry.

Occasionally they would show off a yellow catfish or two that they caught while *noodling*. Noodling meant sticking their hands in holes under water along the banks of the creek and feeling around for a fish. If you felt a fish, you hooked a thumb in its gills and a finger in its mouth and pulled the fish from the water and added to the fisherman's string.

After a few minutes, the spectacle of Thurston and Paul making fools of themselves had quieted, and folks returned to what they were doing. Dad couldn't stand to be around drunks, even funny, good-natured drunks. He was more than ready to load us up in the buggy along with the groceries. Anyway, it was time to head back up the road toward home as it would soon be time to do the evening barn chores and the milking.

It should be noted that my uncle had a heart of gold and completely stopped drinking and worked as a productive carpenter for many years before he passed away from heart failure at the age of 66.

As I sat in my place, scrunched up in the back of the buggy, chewing on my one piece of Double Bubble bubble gum, I tried and tried to blow a bubble with no success. As I worked on the bubble gum, I kept reliving all of the afternoon's events, especially that little yellow airplane on a Saturday afternoon.

END

DOLLY
THE BLIND PONY

From the earliest memories of my childhood, I wanted a pony so badly I could hardly stand it. I wanted a real one, not a pretend stick horse or a broom horse. One of our neighbor's kids, Elma Murdock, had a beautiful brown-and-white pinto pony and I dreamed of having a pony just like hers, complete with a hand-tooled Western bridle and saddle. Her parents owned a large dairy farm, and she rounded up the cows each afternoon for milking. She rode that pony like the wind, her long blonde hair blowing straight out behind her. She was several years older than me, but I think I must have had a crush on her, or maybe it was just the pony. Anyway, when I finally got up enough courage to beg my folks for one, Dad said there were enough critters around the place with mouths to feed, and that included us. I knew better than to bring up any mention of a pony again. I let the issue drop, seeing that when Dad made up his mind about something; that was that, period.

Then late one summer evening a few weeks later, with an hour of daylight left and all the chores done; he suggested that we go for a little ride. "Where are we going?" I asked. He had this mysterious look in his eye, and he almost never burned precious gas to go for a ride. After all, gasoline was almost 30 cents a gallon at the time.

"You'll see," he replied as he, Mother and I piled into the cab of our old '47 Dodge pickup. We traveled a few miles around the twisting gravel road to Lemon's Hill. Topping the hill, we turned right, went through a wooden farm gate and down the narrow dirt lane. We drove past Ernie Hemphill's house to the barn where Ernie was changing the oil in his old Farmall tractor. The old tractor was covered in rust, and the original bright red paint had faded to pink.

After the usual country greetings, Dad got right down to business. "Ernie, I hear tell that you might have a pony for sale."

"Yeah, she belonged to my kids; they're all growed up and gone out on their own, so there ain't much need around here now for the likes of a pony. I don't ride her none, and it just seems like old Dolly just stands around and eats all the time."

"Farm critters do tend to eat; ain't no doubt about that," Dad said with a knowing chuckle.

"'Course now Dolly ain't for sale, mind you, but I'll give her to ya'll if you'll take her off my hands and if Billy here will promise to take good care of her." My heart leaped and nearly burst plum through my chest at the thought that I might finally be getting a pony of my very own, a pony that I could ride like the wind across the cow pasture.

Looking down at me, Ernie ventured, "Now, she's a mite old, Billy. Got 19 years on her as of last month, but she's still got a lot of pep in her step."

"Can we take a look at her?" Dad asked. "Shore thang; let me get her bridle, and I'll get her out of her stable and bring her out here where there's a lot more light. I'll be back with her in a minute."

In a couple of minutes Ernie led Dolly out of the barn hall and into the warm twilight of the summer sunset. Her coat was shaggy and unkempt, but I thought that she was the most beautiful pony I had ever laid my eyes on. Larger than most ponies, she was a beautiful bay color with a black mane and tail. A small white star was in the middle of her forehead and a white stocking on her left front leg.

Dad looked Dolly over carefully, walking her slowly around the barnyard, looking at her teeth, examining her hooves, and finally declaring, "she seems healthy enough, Ernie, but she looks like she's stone blind in both eyes."

"She shore is, has been for years, but that don't hold old Dolly back hardly at all."

"I'll bet she spooks real easy, being blind and all," Dad said. "Nope, she was gentle with the kids before and after she went blind. Never had a problem with her spookin' and running off with any of my young'uns or nothing like that."

"I'm going to have to think about this, Ernie. Can I get back to you tomorrow and let you know if we're going to be interested?"

"Why shore, course you can," Ernie responded as he led Dolly back to the barn hall and her stable.

Dad and Ernie rolled cigarettes and smoked as they talked farming, weather and crops. Mother and Ernie's wife Edie May talked of gardening, canning and who had been eavesdropping on the telephone party line. The conversation lasted until it was full dark before we headed back toward home.

On the way home, all was quiet for the first few minutes except for the gravel crunching under the truck's wheels and a pebble occasionally pinging the truck's undercarriage. Finally, I couldn't stand it any longer. I did something that I knew better than to do. I begged and pleaded with Dad, "Please, please can we bring old Dolly home tomorrow?"

"I don't know right now, son, I really have to think about it. Dolly is old, and she can't see a thing. Plus, she'll eat up her fair share of corn and hay. She ain't like this old truck; it don't eat nothing when it's parked, but she does."

My feathers fell, I was so disappointed that I had to blink the tears back, and for a minute I thought I was going to throw up. I knew that it was hopeless to beg and plead anymore. I could only hope. The next evening, after chores, Dad said, "I suppose we ought to go and get that old blind pony, if you still want her, of course."

At Ernie's, Dad backed the old Dodge up to the loading chute next to the barn, and walked Dolly slowly up the chute and into the truck. Dad closed and latched the tailgate and shook hands with Ernie, closing the deal. I was so happy I thought that I would bust a seam.

On the way home Dad said, "Dolly is your pony and your responsibility, son. If you don't take good care of her, she'll have to go, understood?"

"Yessir."

"It's your job to make sure that she's fed and watered twice a day. I'll get you a brush and currycomb, so you can keep her coat brushed and clean. Make sure she gets plenty of oats to eat, and that will keep her coat healthy and shiny. Of course, you'll need to clean out her stable every couple of days and put down plenty of fresh straw bedding."

I was listening to Dad and I was very quiet. I had only been thinking of how much fun a pony would be, with little thought of the responsibility involved. In a minute my excitement over having a pony returned and replaced any thought or concern of the hard work.

It was almost dark, and a few stars were out when we reached home. Dad drove the old truck around to the back of the barn where there was a clay bank almost the exact same height of the floor of the truck bed, a perfect place to unload Dolly. Once she was in the stable, we watched her for a while to see if she was comfortable in her new surroundings. We wanted to be sure that she wasn't going to get spooked and maybe kick a plank off the barn or hurt herself. She settled down quickly, then moved slowly around the stable until her nose found the feed trough with its ears of corn that she started to munch contentedly. "Looks like Dolly's going to be all right in her new home, son. Let's go get the truck and go to the house."

Dad parked the truck at its regular spot in the gravel driveway, and we walked through the sagging yard gate and around back of the house to the kitchen door and supper on the table. All during supper, I kept interrupting the conversation to say something about my new pony until Dad finally gave me *the look* that said, "That's enough about Dolly."

Mother spoke up, "Oh, Daddy, he's just excited about his new pony. You know how he has always wanted one."

I finally got off to sleep when I went to bed that night, and I don't remember dreaming about anything, even the pony.

The next morning after breakfast and all the regular morning barn chores were done, Dad said, "Let's get Dolly out of her stable, and you can give her a test drive." With her bridle in hand, Dad opened the stable door and quietly called her name. Ears forward, she started to walk slowly toward the sound of his voice. She was a little nervous and whirled away from him a couple of times, going with a snort to the back of the stable. He continued to talk softly until she finally nickered and poked her head out of the stable door. He showed me how to hold her by her chin, force the bit between her teeth, ease the bridle over her ears and buckle it in place. He watched me practice putting on the bridle until he felt comfortable that I had the hang of it.

"She's too tall for you to climb on her back from the ground, son. I'll boost you up this time, but you'll need to climb a fence or find a stump or a windfall that you can use for a step. Always mount her from the left side, that's what she and all horses are used to. If you try to mount up from the wrong side, she's likely to whirl around and try to bite or kick the daylights out of you. You are going to have to use a tow sack as a saddle blanket until we can maybe find an old saddle and a blanket somewhere for you. Now, go ahead and take her for a ride; just be careful—since you're new to her, she might try a *shenanigan* or two, so watch what you're doing and don't fall off." I wasn't sure what shenanigan meant, but I was destined to soon find out.

Old Joe, my black shepherd dog and my constant sidekick, was sitting off to the side watching every move that Dad, this new critter and I were making. Joe's head was tilted to the side as if he was questioning what we were doing. Dad gave me a leg up and said, "Ride Dolly around the calf pasture until you get used to each other; it's flat and open and big enough for Dolly to stretch her legs and for you to get the hang of controlling her." I concentrated on holding the reins in my hands just the way that Dad had shown me and kicked Dolly in the ribs a couple of times. Dolly didn't move a peg; she just snorted a time or two at the little aggravation sitting on her back.

"Kick her harder and holler *giddup*; you have to talk to your pony, son," Dad said. I tried to do as I was told, but I inadvertently leaned forward a bit too far, so that my heels almost kicked her flanks, something that I quickly learned that you don't want to do. Dolly did a grunt, a little bucking jump and took off like greased lightning. Joe gave a couple of quick *yips* and ran alongside me and Dolly, looking up at me, but keeping a safe distance away from the pony's sharp hooves. Dolly's gait wasn't smooth, more like her legs were pogo sticks bouncing me up and down, giving me a bone-jarring ride. I was hanging onto her mane and the reins with both hands, hollering for Dolly "to stop."

"Pull back on the reins and holler 'whoa'!" Dad yelled, for by now I was most of the way across the pasture.

"Whoa, Dolly, whoahhhhhh," I yelled; actually it was more of a scream, but Dolly just kept running, though her gait did start to smooth out some.

We reached the fence line at the backside of the pasture, and somehow I managed to keep her from brushing me off on the fence or running headlong into it. Adding insult to injury, my burlap riding blanket started to slide sideways, taking me with it. I did my best to hang on, but it was no use. I fell off my new pony. I hit the ground so hard that it knocked the breath out of me for a minute or two. My feelings were hurt, and I was embarrassed something fierce, but nothing was broken. Thing was, Dolly stopped in her tracks, dropped her head and nuzzled my face with her velvet nose as if to ask, "are you OK?"

Soon as I was breathing properly again, I led Dolly to a windfall tree nearby and used it as a ladder to get back up on Dolly. This time Dolly and I had a much better understanding of each other, and she slowly walked back to where Dad was. He was standing with his hands on the waist of his overalls, and asked, "You hurt?"

I shook my head, "no," I managed to squeak out, afraid if I said anything I would light right into bawling. "Good thing you found something soft to land on." That day was the beginning of a lasting friendship between me, Dolly and Joe. I suppose that you could say that the three of us *rode together*.

I made sure that Dolly was fed a ration of corn, hay and a cup of oats each night and morning, and that she was watered at the cave spring that ran a small stream just a short distance from the back of the barn. I rode Dolly for fun every day if I had any spare time from doing chores, and Joe was always at our side. In the evening at milking time, rain or shine, I rode Dolly to the pasture to round up the milk cows. Joe did his part, too, helping to herd and nipping the heels of the cows to keep them moving toward the barn.

Several weeks after we brought Dolly home, Dad came back from a trip to the feed store with a used Western pony saddle and saddle blanket. I thought that surely I must have died and gone to heaven. The saddle was scuffed, but with saddle soap and elbow grease, that old saddle was almost good as new. The blanket, once red-and-white striped, was frayed, faded, worn and stained. I didn't mind that, for now I could be a real cowboy even in my overalls, straw hat and work shoes. In my imagination, I was wearing a pair of fancy, pearl-handled six-shooters, cowboy boots and a Western shirt with fringe. I even imagined a white cowboy hat like I had seen Tex Ritter wear in the Saturday matinee movies.

I learned to direct old Dolly with my knees and a light touch of my hand on the reins. Over time, Dolly seemed to gain complete faith in my guidance, and her blindness didn't stop us from running flat out. Problem was her sixth sense sometimes kicked in, and that caused me to take a lot of tumbles. We could be galloping down a familiar cow path after a rain, and if there was the tiniest wash across the path, Dolly would run right up to it and slam on her brakes. She would come to a dead stop, her head down, and her ears snapping forward. Me? I'd go flying over her head to land with a *thud* in the mud or on the hard path. More than a few times I would be knocked cold for a minute or two, then become conscious of Dolly and sometimes Joe, nuzzling my face. They were making sure that I was all right. All the times that I got tossed or thrown, and there were many, I luckily never broke a bone. But I sure had a lot of bruises, and it did hurt my pride. Dolly, Joe and I spent many happy days together, exploring the pastures and woods, rounding up cows and riding the winding country roads of our community.

Then one morning at daylight as usual, I walked down the path to the barn to do my morning chores and to feed old Dolly. It was barely daylight, and I didn't see her at first. I thought she might have gotten out of the stable, but how? The stable door was closed. I think I knew that she was gone even before I saw her lying on the floor of her stable. Her time had finally run out. Dolly had likely died of old age, for by then she was almost 25 years old, and that's really old for a horse or pony. With an unusual act of kindness that I had seldom seen, Dad sent me to the house, and he took care of Dolly's remains. I suppose Joe somehow knew that our friend Dolly was gone. He moped around quietly for several days before he regained his enthusiasm and started to chase rabbits and herd cows again.

Time eventually heals broken hearts, and I eventually came to accept the loss of my old, blind friend. Thing is, if you've ever lived on a farm, you quickly become acquainted with the cycle of life and death, but loss is still painful. I will always remember old Dolly and Joe and all the fun that we had when *we three rode together.*

END

CATALPA SCHOOL

The old grey, weatherworn schoolhouse still sits across from what once had been the thriving Catalpa Country Store. The store building is empty now and has been for years. The old school building has been ravaged by time, neglect and willful destruction. The schoolhouse is ghost-like, sitting well back among the locust trees, blackberry briars and bushes that now cover a large portion of all that remains of the school's campus. Wild grape, honeysuckle and Virginia creeper vines crawl over the outside walls and into the cracks in the weatherboard. Long ago, the old building was painted a pristine white, but now any evidence of paint is gone. The windowpanes are mostly broken, destroyed long ago by bored rock-throwing vandals with too little to keep them busy. Holes in the tin roof, rusted and peeled back by the winds of time, let the rain pour in. One leak has caused a large rotting hole in the ceiling. A section of floor and a part of the small stage at the front of the classroom has collapsed. Even the frames around the cracked and broken blackboards have fallen apart. Beneath the blackboards, a couple of erasers and broken pieces of chalk rest against the wall. A partially erased arithmetic problem remains on the board, almost as a reminder that once this was a place of learning.

There are those that question the validity of ghosts. If you pause in this place for a moment and listen quietly, you can possibly hear the pleasant sounds of laughter and the high, mingled voices of the younger children. Perhaps they're at recess playing simple schoolyard games or answering the teacher's questions in class.

Listen to the crack of a wooden bat and yells of encouragement as the older students play softball and run bases made of limestone rock. Hear the metallic clatter of pitched horseshoes. Are the pleasant ghostly sounds real or imagined? They're all gone now, the real sounds, the voices and the laughter. This is the story of a school I attended that now and forever is relegated to a pleasant memory of a time long gone by.

The school building was "L" shaped and consisted of two large rooms. First was the classroom that we entered from a small covered porch at the front of the building. A bell tower that housed a large school bell topped the porch. A generous length of rope was attached to the bell that dropped through a small hole in the porch ceiling and was looped over a hook on one side wall of the porch. We walked underneath the bell and through the large double front doors. I was always a bit spooked by the bell as I thought it might break loose and fall on me as I walked underneath, but of course that never happened.

Bead board covered the walls and ceiling of the classroom. The walls were pale green, and the ceiling was painted white. The floors were dark and of oiled oak. The older students took turns sweeping the floors and burning the trash at the end of each school day. Natural light came from windows that were down each side of the room and from the six old-fashioned, white electric globes that hung on chains attached to the ceiling. The lights were the only electric fixtures in the entire building.

The classroom entrance was actually at the back of the room, and if you came to class late, you had to face the teacher as you came through the door. Inside, there were two aisles and three rows of old-fashioned desks that ran the length of the room. The desks had uncomfortable flip-up seats and tops made of wood. The top (work surface) of each desk had a 3-inch hole in the upper right-hand corner for an inkwell. Years of flooded fountain pens and spilled ink bottles left map-like permanent ink stains on most of the desks. The tops were carved, scratched, gouged and covered with names and initials of students, sweethearts, even colorful cuss words, all from days long past. The desks had black, wrought-iron bases that were attached to the floor with screws. There were no more than 36 desks total, plus a couple of church pew-type benches at the front of the classroom. A low stage across the front of the room served as a platform for the teacher's desk. A double blackboard covered most of the back wall of the stage. To the left and centered along the stage wall, one small bookcase was filled with mostly children's tattered storybooks. Many books had the hard covers missing, and some had more than a few pages torn out. Another larger bookcase was at the front of the room, next to the stage, and it contained classroom textbooks of history, English, geography, math and literature.

A large old-fashioned, coal-burning stove squatted in an open space at the front of the room, 6 feet from the stage. There was no insulation in the school's wall, so the heat that the stove generated made the room barely tolerable on cold winter days. We sometimes had to keep on our winter coats, caps and earmuffs to keep from freezing. The older boys were kept running back and forth to the coal pile behind the school for another scuttle of coal to stoke the fire and keep it going.

Two outhouses were out behind the school, separated discreetly by their placement in opposite corners at the far backside of the schoolyard. One was for boys, and one was for girls. The boys had a "two holer." I'm not sure if the girls' outhouse had seating for more than one or not. I still don't understand that concept, as I never saw more than one person at a time use either facility.

A rusty, hand-operated pitcher pump was next to an old locust tree, about 25 feet from the front steps of the school. The pump provided drinking water for the entire student body and the kitchen. At recess, the students all got in line. The teacher primed the pump to get the water flowing, and we all took turns at the pump handle until we had a chance to get our drink. Most of us drank out of the same white enamel dipper that hung in its place on a nail driven into the locust tree trunk. I guess passing around a shared dipper was not so unusual in the days of two-room schools. Nowadays, we would probably get sick, curl up and die drinking from a community dipper.

One morning at recess, we were all lined up at the pump as usual to get our drink of water. A storm was brewing, with black clouds moving in. We could hear the rumbling thunder and see lightning flashing in the distance, but our teacher thought the storm was too far away to be of any danger to us. When it came my turn at the dipper, I had just started to get my drink of water, when a lightning bolt struck the locust tree, cutting a huge gash in the trunk. The lightning bounced off the tree and hit the wet dipper, knocking it out of my hand and sending me sprawling. None of the other kids were affected, and other than scaring the hell out of me, I didn't get so much as a scratch. But the dipper was pretty scorched and had a new chip in the enamel. Some of the older kids swore that for just a second there was a green halo around my entire body, but I was never sure if they were serious. I do know one thing: The experience encouraged me to show a lot more appreciation for my guardian angels.

Kenneth Brown was the school's only teacher during the time I attended school at Catalpa. He pulled the school bell rope every morning, ringing the warning bell at 7:45 a.m. You were expected to be in your seat and ready for class when the bell rang again promptly at 8:00 a.m. If you were late to class and without a good excuse, you were marked tardy in the roll book and sent home for the day. Three unexcused tardies got you expelled for a week or an opportunity to endure a severe paddling in front of the class; the choice was yours.

All the classes, first through eighth grade, were taught in this one large, open classroom. Each class (usually with no more than five or six students) moved to the front of the room and sat on the church pew-type benches in front of the teacher's desk when it came their class time. The rest of the students were expected to do homework or sit quietly and listen to the class in progress.

My mother had taught me to read by the time I was 5, mostly to keep me busy and out from underfoot, I suspect. At school, I sometimes read one of the children's books from the little bookcase or listened as I drew airplanes, cars, bulldozers and trucks all over the pages of my Blue Horse ruled tablet. I always seemed to be reading or drawing something, even at that early age. I did listen most of the time to the lessons for each class, although much of the material was way beyond my comprehension. Still I absorbed a lot from a combination of reading the library books plus listening to the other students in class. I learned by reading, listening, observing and participating. I suppose it could be said that what I learned came partially from osmosis. By the time that I entered the third grade, I had read or studiously flipped through almost all of the "library" books, and since extra textbooks were available, I read many of those, too.

The building's other room, which formed an "L" off the classroom, was a combination kitchen and cafeteria. Two long tables were covered in brightly colored oilcloth with benches to sit on. The food was served family-style with bowls of food placed on the tables, and you could eat all you wanted for the price of 25 cents. Mrs. Sally Will Hemphill was the cook, and she served up some terrific Southern home cooking from a big wood-burning stove. There was no electricity for a refrigerator, and anything she served was either fresh or home-canned. Water for cooking came from the outside pitcher pump that we all drank from. We could hear the old pump squeaking as Miss Sally Will pumped water for the kitchen.

Great smells from the kitchen floated through the classroom when it was close to lunchtime, making us all hungry and temporarily distracting us from our work. I didn't have much of an opportunity to eat "Miss Sally Will's" good cooking, as my family couldn't afford the 25 cents that the lunch cost each day. Mother packed my lunch in a brown grocery bag, and it was usually potted meat or sliced Vienna sausage and Miracle Whip Salad Dressing on Merita light bread. Sometimes she would add a slice of country ham or sausage on a biscuit, left over from breakfast. For dessert, I might have a fried peach pie or a piece of Mother's wonderful chocolate meringue pie.

Although I knew better than to let on to my folks, I was embarrassed by having to take my lunch to school because none of the other kids did. I usually found a place where I could hide and eat my lunch—somewhere on the school grounds, behind the school, a tree or scrub undergrowth. I didn't realize at the time that my lunch was packed with love each and every day, and the food that I was embarrassed to eat in plain view would be considered "gourmet" today in my estimation.

As I mentioned, we didn't have a lot of money at our house, and Mother, using an old-fashioned foot-treadle sewing machine, sewed my overalls out of denim material and my shirts out of cotton-print feed bags or flour sacks. My classmates were amazed at Mother's ingenuity and thought it was so great that my mother actually made all my clothes, especially my overalls. I was embarrassed that I didn't have store-bought clothes like everyone else in school. Oh, the foolishness and ignorance of youth!

I started to school when I was 5, not that I was particularly intelligent but because the county school board was about to close the school due to low attendance, and the Catalpa Community was doing everything it could to keep the little school open. During the time that I attended Catalpa School, there were only 18 to 20 regular students in the entire school. I attended the first, second and the beginning of the third grade before the county was finally forced to close down the school for good because there were only 14 students. There was something wonderfully unique in having the opportunity to attend that two-room school and experience all eight grades in the big open classroom.

As mentioned earlier, our teacher was Kenneth Brown, a 19-year-old college student that lived with his folks on a farm less than three-quarters of a mile down the road from the school. He and most of the students lived close enough to walk to school unless the weather was really bad. Kenneth was an excellent, dedicated teacher and really cared that we learned. If you were around him for any length of time, you would find that he was a wonderful person, but he was tough in the classroom and a strict disciplinarian. He was fair…and like many of those who dwell in my childhood memories, he left a positive and lasting impression on my life.

He believed in liberal use of the old-fashioned paddle and kept one hanging on a nail on the side of his desk. More than once, he sent an unruly older boy out to cut a switch that Kenneth would use to whip him. He drew a circle on the blackboard for the girls and smaller kids when they acted up. I did my share of standing on one foot with my nose in the ring for what seemed like an eternity.

Funny how when we're older, we still remember some of the smallest things that people do that become positive forces in our lives. Somehow we're more prone to remember the good instead of the bad; thank goodness. Small things from our childhood experiences become magnified and can be so lasting that they literally help shape us. What follows are a couple of those seemingly small, but memorable, things that Kenneth did for me that I've never forgotten. In the wintertime, I was sick a lot with colds and allergies and missed too many school days. So many, in fact, that I was on the verge of failing first grade for lack of attendance. Kenneth would leave my lesson assignments at the Catalpa store for my Dad to bring home. The problem was that Dad didn't get to the store every day to pick up or drop off my homework, so Kenneth would walk from the schoolhouse passing the Catalpa store and turning down the dirt and gravel lane for the three-quarters of a mile trip, and at least half of it uphill, to our house, rain, shine or snow with my homework. He would spend time going over each lesson, making sure that I understood the assignments before he left our house.

December of that year brought snow and ice, lots of it. I was in the second grade. And once again I was sick with a lingering cold. Kenneth, not wanting me to miss out on the exchange of Christmas gifts at school, climbed our hill through the mud and snow to deliver my presents. The small packages were all wrapped in bright Christmas paper, and each was tied with a red ribbon and bow. One of the gifts was a toy Army tank, made of fiberboard and painted gray. The only part of the tank that moved was a removable gun turret. The tank was filled with hard Christmas candy in bright colored wrappers. In the other package was a coloring book, a tray of watercolors and a small brush.

Kenneth had purchased the gifts with his own money so that I wouldn't feel left out. The toys were inexpensive but to me they were the most wonderful gifts. I kept the little toy tank for years until it finally disintegrated. I wasn't special or singled out; he would have done the same for any of his students. I'm sure he did. That's just the way Kenneth was, and you never forget the caring, kindness and generosity of people like that. Kenneth had a great sense of humor and often made it a point in more recent years of inviting me to come by his house for supper "to sit and watch him eat steak."

For me, every school day was filled with excitement and fun; we had plenty to do in and out of class. For recreation at recess and at lunch, we played games: softball, fox-in-the-morning-goose-in-the-evening, red rover or horseshoes. The first-grade and second-grade boys even occasionally played "house" with the girls!

Most afternoons, when school let out, we would head straight to Wade's store, which was across the road from the southeast corner of the schoolyard. We would hang out, and if we had a nickel or two to spend, we would munch on Planters peanuts that we had poured into bottles of NeHi Orange or old-fashioned

Cokes. The old original "Co-colas" would burn your nose and make your eyes water with every swallow. Cold drinks finished, conversations done, and our farm chores looming, we would each start our long walk home. I would leave the store and turn down the dusty lane a hundred yards east. The lane led me by Wade's house, barn and the big old pear tree that grew in his small pasture. Farther down the lane, I crossed over a stock gap and made my way past Freeman Wakefield's house and dairy barn. I continued on, going through two gates that were across the lane and finally up the long hill, past a large elm tree, and through the front gate to our yard. Looking back now, that seems to be a fairly long walk for a 5 or 6 year old, but that time by myself gave my imagination time to grow.

Each day, my walk to and from school was filled with new adventures and discoveries for a small boy out on his own for the first time. In the spring, all sorts of wild flowers, including Black-eyed Susan, butterfly weed and red clover, grew in profusion all along the roadside. The farm fields belonging to Bob Murdock on the east side of the road were green and red with the blooming crimson clover that would later be cut as hay for his big dairy herd of black-and-white Holstein cows. Big yellow-and-black swallowtail butterflies, fat bumblebees, noisy meadowlarks and red-winged blackbirds were everywhere. An electric fence surrounded the Murdock's field to keep the cows in, and one afternoon, when not a soul was in sight, I made the mistake of taking a "leak" on that fence, and to my rather painful surprise, it was a real shocking "experience." I didn't have to be told to never do that again.

On my way home, I had to walk across an old rickety wooden bridge with loose boards that would rattle noisily when a car or truck crossed. The little creek that ran underneath the bridge was crystal clear and filled with tadpoles, minnows, small sunperch and suckerfish. There were crayfish and fascinating rocks, all sorts of things to capture the interest and the attention of a 5-year-old boy on his way to or from school.

The old pear tree that stood out behind Wade's house was close to the road and way too tempting for me to ignore, especially when it was loaded down with hard, wonderfully sweet, pears. In the late fall I made it a practice to climb over the fence every afternoon on the way home and help myself to those big green pears, until finally Wade put a stop to it. He didn't mind my stealing the pears so much, but mashing his wire fence down, letting his beef cow out, did bother him somewhat. He mentioned it to Dad, and my fence-climbing, pear-stealing days were over.

Wade cured me from stealing at an early age. One of my friends, Bobby Welch, and I discovered a hen nest atop an old wheat thresher in a shed attached to the blacksmith shop owned by Bobby's uncles, Joe and Leonard Welch. We gathered the eggs, and since Bobby was older, naturally, I was elected to be the one to take them to Wade's store. I intended to trade the eggs for candy and Co-colas, but instead of candy, Bobby and me got the third degree. You would have thought that we had broken into Fort Knox as Wade chewed us out something fierce, and then called our parents. I don't know about Bobby, but I got my rear end worn out and a stern lecture when I got home. Another time I emptied my clear glass piggybank of $10 that I had saved, with the intention of spending it all at one time on bananas. I had never had my fill of bananas, but Wade put a stop to that too. He refused to sell me any bananas and promptly called my folks. It's really too bad that people don't watch out for other people's kids the way they once did.

The county school board closed Catalpa School just before I was to start the third grade, and all the kids were transferred to different schools. I was supposed to go to school in Petersburg, but it took Mother and me three months to convince Dad that I should go to school somewhere. He was of the opinion that if I couldn't go to school in my community, I shouldn't go at all.

After much crying and begging on my part, and some rational arguments from Mother, we finally wore him down, and he gave in. That's the only time I remember him giving in to anything, ever. I was to attend Petersburg Elementary School, which was about 8 miles from where we lived. I met the other neighborhood kids at Catalpa store; then we had to walk almost 2 miles east on Catalpa road to catch the school bus. Twice daily, the bus traveled 75 miles over country roads to pick up kids for delivery to Petersburg Elementary and Morgan High School and then take them home at the end of the school day.

The Catalpa school is gone. Kenneth has passed away. Wade and his country store are no more. Most of the people that I knew in this little farming community are gone, either moved away or have passed on to their eternal reward. Even the landscape doesn't look the same anymore. Many of the once prosperous and well-maintained farms are all grown over with bushes and weeds, and too many of the buildings have been neglected and are falling down.

But there will always be in my fondest memories, Kenneth Brown, Catalpa School, Wade's store and the good people that were the Catalpa community of my childhood. They are way more than friends; they're family and always will be.

I ran across this line in a book the other day that might say it best:

We are drawn to people, not so much for who they are but for the positive way they make us feel about ourselves.

END

DECORATION DAY — DOWN SOUTH

The year was 1944, and it had been unseasonably hot and dry for May. The cars coming from the east and west on the dirt roads kicked up billowing clouds of dust that choked, burned the eyes and filled the air like a thick tan fog. Still, I had a 5-year-old's sense of anticipation. We were going to Decoration Day, all-day singing and dinner-on-the ground at Center Point United Methodist Church in the small community of Beech Hill, Tennessee. I had never been to a Decoration Day that I could remember, but I thought that it had to be something good because we were all dressed up in our Sunday clothes and my mother's wonderful cooking was involved.

I was sitting in the back seat of Dad's old Model A Ford. Next to me on the seat was a cardboard box emitting the most wonderful aromas. The box contained still-warm fried chicken, country ham, butter beans, fried corn, spoon biscuits and home-made coconut cake, all of which Mother had prepared, starting before daylight that morning. A dish towel covered the box in an effort to keep out the road dust and the ever-present houseflies of summer. The car windows were rolled down to catch what little air that was stirring, but we caught a lot more dust than air.

Mother was wearing one of her homemade print dresses. A pert white hat with a veil sat jauntily on her head. Daddy's brown Sunday slippers were polished to such a shine that you could see yourself in them. Mother and I were already sweat-soaked and caked with dust, but Daddy, as always, looked cool and crisp, seemingly without a speck of dust or a bead of sweat anywhere. He was in his Sunday best, a broad-brimmed white Panama hat, white shirt, his special tie and the one pair of tan dress pants that he owned. Mother had me put on my "dress-up" short-sleeved white shirt, seersucker short pants and Red Goose shoes.

Folks came from near and far, some from as far as 25 miles away to attend the annual homecoming and to enjoy the all-day Decoration Day festivities.

Vehicles all covered in dust, parked in the church parking area or turned in at the open gate that was the cemetery entrance and parked in a grassy area. Folks already parked were walking from their cars and trucks carrying baskets and cardboard boxes of food. They added their contributions to a rapidly filling picnic table. Some of the more well-off folks brought their food in wicker picnic baskets. The table of rough-sawn lumber was covered with an oilcloth that had a pattern of brightly colored fruit. The table was in the shade of big oak trees in one corner of the cemetery. The food was like the best of Sunday dinners, which included fresh-cooked vegetables, fried chicken, roast beef and ham, home-made corn bread, biscuits and rolls. There were more pies, cakes and cobblers than you could count.

Daddy kept our food box in the car for some unknown reason, preferring to eat just the food we brought instead of sharing like everyone else. I never understood why—Mother's cooking was the best there ever was. I guess that Daddy just didn't want to go sharing it with all those other folks.

We did join with the folks as they gathered to sing in the church, finding hard seats next to the back row of pews. The church house was a little cooler than the outside, with three or four fans hanging from the ceiling, all with spinning blades. Plus, the air had the additional benefit of being stirred by the womenfolk with their hand-held cardboard fans. One side of the fan featured a color picture of Jesus in the Garden, and the other side advertised Russell Massey's Funeral Home in the nearby town of Boons Hill.

While families were still streaming through the doors of the little white church, filling the pews; voices were filling the air with the sweet comforting sound of old country church hymns. Ms. Robbie Coffee, who was rich and beautiful, played the piano. I knew that she was rich because she had a fancy comb in her hair, and she wore a fancy shawl over a long black dress with big pink flowers. The singing continued for over an hour; then folks broke for lunch at high noon. As all the other folks were making their way to the big table to eat, we headed for our old car. I thought that it was a good thing that Daddy had parked in the shade.

We all bowed our heads while the preacher said grace. Mother got plates, silverware, glasses and cloth napkins out of the box and served up the food to me and Daddy right proper-like. The three of us sat on the running board of the car as we ate and watched the actions of the rest of the folks. Ms. Della Maye Wakefield came by, showing off her special lemon meringue pie, already sliced, and offered us a piece. Daddy said that it was okay to have a piece if I wanted. He and mother both accepted slices, and Mother offered Della Maye several slices of her coconut cake, which she took. The preaching and singing commenced again at 1:30 p.m., but instead of joining in the singing, Mother, Daddy and I put flowers on my grandparents' (Daddy's parents') grave. They didn't have a gravestone, but the grave location was marked by a big cedar tree. Then we walked around to look at how other folks had decorated their family's graves.

I asked Mother why there were so many Holley family members buried at Center Point. Some of the gravestones even had a photo of the person resting there. "Because your daddy's family migrated from North Carolina and settled this area over a hundred years ago. A lot of the descendants of the original Holley clan still live around here," she replied. After looking at a bunch more gravestones, and Daddy and Mother striking up a conversation with several folks that they knew, Daddy pulled his pocket watch from his pocket to check the time. "It's 3:30 p.m.; I guess we'd better load up and head for home. Them old cows will be wondering where we are."

TIME GOES SWIFTLY BY...

I haven't been to Center Point for Decoration Day and dinner on the ground in more years than I'd like to remember. I don't know if they still get together, but I sure hope they do. Everyone that I knew there has either moved away or passed on. Even the old cedar tree that marked my grandparents' grave is gone and the stump rotted away.

On the third Sunday in May, for many years now, my wife Beverly and I make the 75-mile trip south to attend Decoration Day services at the rural Talley Cemetery in the farming community of Catalpa, Tennessee. My family lived in the community for several years when I was small.

My parents are buried there as well as an uncle, aunt and a host of other relatives and friends, those that were close and a few maybe not so close. These are the folks that I knew as a child growing up in this once close-knit farming community. The cemetery was so named because the Talley ancestors donated the land, long before the unfortunate incident of the Civil War. A large number of Talley folks are buried there.

The cemetery is on a slight rise, and from this vantage point, looking toward the southwest, you can see the little white farmhouse high on the hill where my folks and I lived for four or five years. Here, as a sharecropper, Dad farmed the hillsides with a team of mules and a hillside turning plow. This was back in the mid to late 1940s.

Decoration Day is a unique Southern tradition that, I am told, was originally started to give pause to remember and respect the memory of those who fought and died in the Civil War—a cause they truly believed in. Later it became a time of remembrance for all of those who fought and died defending our country. A celebration of the lives of those who thought the American way of life and freedom were worth fighting and dying for.

Today, Decoration Day has become a time to gather together and hold simple services that last only a couple of hours, at most. And a time to place flowers on the graves of those who rest there.

If celebrated at all in other parts of the country—Decoration Day has morphed into Memorial Day. We still celebrate at Talley Cemetery even though there is no church, no all-day singing and no dinner on the ground. In reality, Decoration Day is a family and community reunion, an opportunity to visit with family members and old friends, some that they probably haven't seen since Decoration Day last year or in years further back.

The service was to start promptly at 2:00 p.m. as it had every Decoration Day that I could remember. Most folks were already there, on time and cars parked, but a few latecomers, including my wife and I, pulled in and quickly parked with only minutes to spare.

As always seemed to be the case, it was an unusually hot, steamy Sunday afternoon in late May. The rain that moved through that morning had only served to increase the humidity, and that made the steaming heat feel even more pronounced. A few of the men were dressed in suits; some were outdated fashion statements. White shirts and ties askew, they looked on the whole, totally uncomfortable and ill at ease. Most of the women were dressed in their Sunday best. Once upon a time everyone dressed up in his or her "Sunday best" to attend Decoration Day, but not so much any more.

There were blue jeans, short-sleeved sport shirts and T-shirts present now. Even a few overalls were in attendance. I don't think the casual dress is such a bad thing. I know that it had to be a lot more comfortable than a suit and tie. I miss the dress-up formality slightly I suppose, but I was sweating in my suit, beads of sweat making rivulets down my face and my back. I was a definite member of the suit-wearing "uncomfortable set." Maybe next year I'll wear a sport shirt and a pair of jeans, too.

Approximately 50 to 60 people attended the service. Every age, from toddlers to 80-year-old great–grandparents, were there. Some seemed to be in deep conversation as they slowly gravitated from the graves to the shade of a big maple tree that grew in an open area near the entrance of the cemetery. A scattering of folks was still wandering among the tombstones, placing the pretty, bright-colored bouquets of real and artificial flowers on the graves and headstones of their friends and loved ones.

Years ago, the graves were hand-dug by neighbors and friends, using a pick and shovel. For the men doing the work, it was showing a sign of deep respect for the deceased and their family. Now the entire grave-digging process is done quickly and efficiently, with a backhoe. Efficiency is important and necessary, I suppose, but with every improvement, something valuable seems to get lost forever.

Beverly and I placed our flowers on the family gravestones or on the graves. Now, looking across the field of tombstones, the entire cemetery was awash with bright colors. Whether the flowers are fresh-cut, silk or Wal-Mart plastic, it doesn't matter. They are placed with the same gentleness and respect, each person pausing to make sure the bouquets are positioned "just right." It looked as though there were flowers "blooming in profusion" on every grave in the cemetery.

Some folks had already placed flowers on graves early that morning, having their own reasons for not wanting to attend the services that afternoon. And for some this is a return visit after several years of being absent. They walk slowly from stone to stone, seeming to be in thought, stopping to read the names and the special inscriptions chiseled into the granite.

Visitors stand quietly now, lost in memories and thoughts, silent with respect. Everyone has finally gathered in the shade. A tear trickles down a face here and there. A few white handkerchiefs can be seen scattered throughout the crowd.

Kenneth Brown, the white-haired, 80-year-old chairman of the cemetery "board of directors," makes his way through the gathering, passing a hat and talking up the annual donations. The cost of keeping the cemetery mowed keeps going up every year. "Dig deep," he admonishes. Salt-of-the-earth farm folks, factory workers and those of us who left the farm long ago for a life in the city reach into our pockets to give what we can to pay those hired to do the upkeep. There is no charge to be buried at Talley Cemetery if you have family members already buried there. It is financially operated on donations and a trust fund only. The secretary-treasurer passes out a one-sheet "annual report" every year. "The board," those who manage the graveyard and the upkeep, are all volunteers. After Kenneth collects the dollars and the checks, he sternly reminds the crowd to check family headstones. Some have come dangerously close to falling over, and many already have. Kenneth at the age of 18 was my first grade school teacher. He was a wonderful, thoughtful and compassionate man and a dear friend. Unfortunately, Kenneth left us a few years ago.

While the hat is being passed, the song leader announces the song, hums to get the pitch, and starts to sing the old hymn, "In the Garden." We all join in; some are really off-key; but we all give it our best. I wondered to myself, slightly amused, if we were all singing the same song. At least we were loud, and our hearts were in the right place. With the "business" part of the service completed on time, everyone forms a loose circle as the rest of today's program is verbally outlined by the preacher.

A clean-cut young man stands off to one side and slightly out of the circle with his wife and baby. His father had been buried at Talley less than a week before, and he had been asked to give the opening prayer. His dad was a good friend of mine, and we had attended school together. I had known him almost all of my life. I missed his funeral, as I didn't know of his passing until it was too late.

After the prayer, there was a short talk by the local Church of Christ preacher. His words aren't fancy or eloquent, just honest, from the heart. The songs are from church hymnals that have seen a lot of years and a lot of use. These were borrowed from the Catalpa Church of Christ just down the road west of the cemetery, as they have been every year for as long as I can remember.

Again, the song leader makes no introduction to what we will sing. He hums for a second or two to get on key, and then he just starts singing, "The Little Brown Church in the Wildwood." Voices add as the crowd joins in, some still off-key, some loudly nasal, some too low, some too loud, but all somehow coming together to make the old church songs never sound better.

After the preacher's talk, the song leader leads us in two more songs; another prayer was said; and the secretary-treasurer announces that $6,000.00 has been collected for cemetery upkeep. After the announcement about finances, we were dismissed from the formal service.

Several small groups formed, old friends and distant relatives (and some not so distant) catching up on their lives and their current condition. Many only see each other at this once-a-year event. As Beverly and I made our way through the small groups, visiting with those that we knew and introducing ourselves to those we didn't, I realized that we actually knew fewer and fewer people each year that we attended. Many of my life-long friends were now buried here, and third and fourth generations were now attending Decoration Day to honor them. I made a mental note of some of those who were missing from the small gathering this year, and of the graves that were not there the previous year on Decoration Day.

It got me to wondering just how many of my friends, family and acquaintances were buried in this little country cemetery. It was a reminder to me that each year my circle of old friends, former neighbors and family is getting smaller and smaller, until most are gone now. I made a vow to myself not to wait another year to visit these grounds and get a list before the next Decoration Day. My curiosity was quietly working overtime. I realize that as the years pass by, we all lose our loved ones at an ever-increasing rate.

Standing there in the shade of the tree, during the simple ceremony of love and respect, I thought what a wonderful bit of this country's tapestry has been woven at this moment in time. Will it continue to be repeated year after year, long into the future as generations get further and further removed from those resting at Talley Cemetery and Center Point? Will this wonderful tradition fade away, as have so many other simple traditional values of southern rural America? What happens to the memories of the lives of those whose very existence is now marked only with a granite stone, a sinking 3-by-6-foot rectangle of ground ... and dust? I wonder, will there be a Decoration Day at Talley next year?

...I still miss those wonderful dinners on the ground at Center Point. Maybe we'll go back next year.

END

RAINDROPS

It's been powerful hot these last few days of late July. Been cutting and baling hay and sweatin' for weeks now. Just finished putting the final bale in the hay barn and the tractor and hay baler in the shed a few minutes ago. Good thing, too, as there's a black thundercloud rolling over the hills from the west and heading our way. Our strongest summer storms always seem to come from out of the west.

The wind that's pushing ahead of the storm is stirring up the dust of the barnyard, creating whirling dust devils that grab my attention as they pick up leaves and bits of trash, spinning them higher and higher in the air to finally fall back to earth. As the dark clouds roll closer, I watch as jagged lightning bolts flash all across the sky, dancing to the sharp claps as the thunderbolts strike. The air cools, and the sound gets louder and louder as it comes closer. The thunder rumbles and rolls as if God himself is reprimanding all who can hear and bear witness. It's a wonderful, scary, heavenly light show complete with ear-splitting sound effects and earth-shattering vibrations that once again remind me of Old Mother Nature's awesome power.

Ahhhhh, here I sit in this old, paint-chipped, front porch swing, with a freshly brewed hot cup of coffee in hand, watching this magnificent scene playing out before my eyes. I love the thunderstorms of summer, always have. I love the intensty and how it cools the air on a hot day. How it waters the thirsty summer earth and makes things grow. How it reminds me of how small and finite that we really are in nature's scheme of things. To me, it's like standing on a beach and looking at the vastness of the ocean. Of course, I love sunny days too, but there's something magical and surreal about the drama and beauty that plays out across the sky during a summer thunderstorm. I inhale deeply, smelling the freshness of the coming rain. I hear the first few drops as they clatter on the tin roof of my front porch. I watch as the big drops start their *plop, plop, plop* in the powdery tan dust of the barnyard, as they weave a random pattern of dark brown splotches across the open area, soon blending together in chocolate brown muddy unity.

As the drops increase, the rain on the roof becomes a constant roar.

The random *splat* of those big liquid drops quickly turns into the quick-stepping tap dance of a downpour. The old Rhode Island Red rooster and his barnyard hen harem cluck nervously as they scratch the earth one last time before they run, wings all aflutter, for the safety of the dry barn hall and the chicken house. My mind is in neutral as I clasp the warm coffee cup in both hands. I gaze at the crystal droplets as they form and crawl down the windowpanes. Each drop going at its own pace, charts its course, fast at first, then almost coming to rest, before speeding on its journey again. Another drop follows in hot pursuit, then another and another, each taking the path of the one that came before it.

It's always been awe-inspiring to me to see how all things green and growing reach thirstily toward the heavens to welcome the life-giving raindrops. How after a long dry spell, the yellow poplars' leaves turn their underside out and rattle with joy, in the breeze that always comes just before the rain.

As I sit here on the porch watching it rain, I get to thinking about the nature of things that we mostly take for granted, especially about those little raindrops.

A few nights ago, I read an article that some feller wrote about Einstein's theory of relativity and his thoughts pertaining to quantum physics. Now, I don't know a danged thing about that stuff, but I do know that we humans have been on a search since we thought the first thought trying to get a handle on who we are, where we came from, and what we're doing here in the first place. There are all sorts of ideas about how the universe, or multiples of such, were created.

In this same article another *mathematical genius* says that it was a well-ordered and planned set of events set in motion and created by the "big bang" that caused the creation of the cosmos... then in almost the same breath, this genius says that since this is true, there is no reason to believe that a divine force planned and is in charge of this whole production.

That feller is full of contradictory bull pucky as far as I'm concerned, and I have to wonder about the atheists and agnostics who have the audacity to think that this whole great and marvelous creation was "just an accident, the result of random forces." How can there be a total solar system that is mathematically precise, down to the last tiny neutron, without some all-powerful force, guiding the galaxies and this little round ball we call Earth as it all spins through the universe?

Einstein believed in the *energy of the universe* as the guiding force and a force for good but not a divine being (God). Kind of an all-powerful energy that runs through all of us, I suppose. An energy force that set this whole thing in motion, then stepped back to let things run on their own, including our own evolution from a single cell, or something to that effect. Like I said, I didn't understand what I was reading, but in my opinion Einstein was sort of on the right track except for nature's energy force and the stepping back to let it happen part. It seems to me that he was talking out of both sides of his mouth at the same time.

Funny how that simple little drop of rain is a magical, wondrous thing that never really goes away, like everything else on this earth. It just changes to steam rising from the earth on a hot day, or a drop of dew on an early spring morning, or fog after a summer rainstorm. It could become part of a cloud mass that will drop rain in another part of this old world.

That little raindrop is just a part of the perfect system of the universe, galaxy or cosmos, or whatever you want to call it. The mere idea of it all is so overwhelming that we just can't get our heads around it no matter how hard we try, and we do try, and try, and try...then we make up what we don't know and treat it as fact.

Right now, my brain is starting to hurt from all this thinking and wondering. Guess I'll sit back in this old front porch swing, enjoy my coffee, and watch as God paints the miracle of this thunderstorm across his heavenly canvas and wonder how those little raindrops making their way down the windowpane figured out how to get to where they're going.

END

ABOUT THE AUTHOR

Bill Holley was born in southern Middle Tennessee in 1939. His parents were sharecroppers, and he was their only child. His family moved five times within a fifteen-mile radius in the first 10 years of his life. He spent his early life jumping creeks, doing farm chores, exploring nature and playing with friends, both real and imaginary. Holley left the farm as a young adult, shaped by his unique environment, experiences and influences. He went to school, studied art and design, and spent forty-nine years with the prestigious Nashville, Tennessee ad agency, The Buntin Group. In 2000, Holley joined an elite group of prominent and distinguished advertising executives when he was named NAF Silver Medalist by the Nashville Advertising Federation. He has been honored with numerous Addy awards, but is perhaps most noted for his design of the iconic Cracker Barrel logo. Holley is a commissioned artist skilled in various mediums, including water-color, acrylic and oil, and is an accomplished photographer. He thrives in the outdoors, loves to garden, walk the woods, read, write and cook. He has two adult daughters, two sons-in-law, a cat "Pusskits", a granddog "Frog", and a grandcat "Sushi." He lives with his wife Beverly, of fifty-one years, in Franklin, Tennessee, and is at work on a second collection of stories.

IN PRAISE OF *FLOUR SACK SHIRTS & HOMEMADE JAM*

Bill, your stories are wonderful! You have a gift of describing the setting so well that I feel as if I've been transported there and I'm witnessing the very events unfold. I see the smiling people, I smell the aromas of the fresh baked food and the fragrance of the wild blooms, and I hear the voices, especially the ones addressing you as "Billy." Thank you for your efforts in capturing these wonderful memories that also take me back to my own childhood.

– Barbara D.

You either have an INCREDIBLE memory or a great writer's eye for detail. You have a real knack. I could visualize the entire "lay of the land." But it really is the details that stand out. The description of the landscape. The paw paw fruit. Even the description of people ("...tall, slightly stooped and gaunt with thinning gray hair and a drooping, slightly tobacco-stained, walrus mustache that matched the color of his hair, but for the stains...").

– Kerry O

I really liked the story about Delina. Every detail rang true and you could have completely convinced me it was written the day after it happened. It was very believable and a great story! I am particularly fond of historical fiction which requires the writer to immerse you in another time and place. I think your story is really successful in that way. I like that I could really visualize everything you described and felt like your artistic strengths probably brought that "imagery" to life in the story. This one really feels like the first in a number of stories about the characters you introduced. I immediately wanted to read an additional story about your Uncle Brown and Paul Hawkins adventures!

– Donna R.

CPSIA information can be obtained at www.ICGtesting.com
Printed in the USA
LVOW13s1700301113

363343LV00005B/8/P